TEXAS INSTRUMENTS

Graphing Calculator
Strategies

Algebra

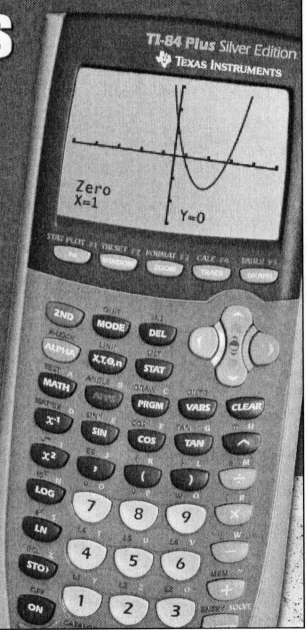

TI-84 Plus Silver Edition
TEXAS INSTRUMENTS

Zero
X=1   Y=0

TI-83/84 Plus Family
& TI-73 Explorer

Author

Pamela H. Dase, M.A.ED
Recipient of PAESMEM
and
Certified National T³ Instructor

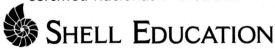
SHELL EDUCATION

Editor
Karie Feldner Gladis, M.S.Ed.

Assistant Editor
Torrey Maloof

Editorial Director
Emily R. Smith, M.A.Ed.

Editor-in-Chief
Sharon Coan, M.S.Ed.

Editorial Manager
Gisela Lee, M.A.

Creative Director
Lee Aucoin

Cover Designer
Amy Couch

Illustration Manager
Timothy J. Bradley

Imaging
Phil Garcia
Sandra Riley
Don Tran

Publisher
Corinne Burton, M.A.Ed.

Shell Education
5301 Oceanus Drive
Huntington Beach, CA 92649-1030
www.shelleducation.com
ISBN-978-1-4258-0024-6
© 2007 Shell Education
Reprinted, 2007
Made in U.S.A.

Table of Contents

Table of Contents *(cont.)*

Introduction

Introduction

Notes

Research Base

Teachers of mathematics have the dual challenge of managing the varying dynamics of their diverse classrooms as well as increasing student achievement across a wide range of mathematical concepts and skills. In the various mathematical subject areas, the TI Graphing Calculator can be an important tool that teachers introduce to their students in order to meet these challenges. With proper use, graphing calculators can meet the needs of all students by promoting higher levels of thinking, increasing student performance in math, and allowing access to mathematical exploration, experimentation, and enhancement of mathematical concepts (Waits and Pomerantz 1997). Graphing calculators were first introduced in 1986 by Casio and started a dynamic change in the way that mathematics was taught and learned (Waits and Demana 1998). As these tools improved and as researchers studied their effectiveness in mathematical instruction, well-known mathematical organizations, such as the National Council of Teachers of Mathematics (NCTM), have recommended that the appropriate types of calculators be used in math instruction from kindergarten through college (NCTM 2000). However, the tool will not achieve the lofty goals that educators have for student success all by itself. It is not enough to simply provide students with graphing calculators. Teachers need access to research-based effective strategies that they can employ for comprehensive mathematics instruction using the technology (NCTM 2003).

TI Graphing Calculator Strategies, Algebra offers the necessary foundation for teachers to translate simple calculator use into actual student comprehension of mathematical concepts, as well as the ability to perform mathematical skills. With the lessons provided in this book, teachers are given valuable techniques for integrating the TI Graphing Calculator into their instruction.

TI Graphing Calculator Strategies, Algebra directs teacher instruction in maximizing student use of the graphing calculators while processing and learning algebraic concepts.

The lessons in this book are designed to give new and veteran teachers the best strategies to employ. How well students understand mathematics, their ability to use it to work out problems, and their confidence and positive attitudes toward mathematics are all shaped by the quality of the teaching they encounter in school (NCTM 2005). Teachers no longer have to construct well-planned calculator lessons unaided. Besides lesson descriptions and materials lists, this book offers step-by-step instructions for four key instructional phases: Explaining the Concept, Using the Calculator, Applying the Concept, and Extension Ideas. Each element has an easily identified icon, and when appropriate, the elements are combined for maximum learning of a particular math concept.

The TI Graphing Calculator Strategies, Algebra lessons move students from concrete understanding of mathematical concepts through the abstract comprehension level, and finally to real-life application, while at the same time allowing students to develop graphing calculator skills. For teaching to be effective in a mathematics classroom, it is necessary to provide focused instruction that moves the student from the concrete to the abstract to the application of the concept (Marzano 2003). In the **Explaining the Concept** portion of each lesson, conceptual development is provided by integrating the use of manipulatives and hands-on activities before and during calculator use. Often with typical calculator instruction, the focus is purely on the procedure; however, research has shown that it is ineffective to emphasize a high degree of procedural proficiency without developing conceptual knowledge (Marzano 2003; Sutton and Krueger 2002). Graphing calculators can build on conceptual understanding by allowing students to practice numerous representations of concepts and experiences in a way that is not possible by paper and pencil alone. As a result of these methods, teachers are able to engage students more effectively by addressing different learning styles and developing understanding that leads to higher-level thinking. Teachers do not often associate the use of graphing calculators with the conceptual process. When students use concrete objects to represent mathematical ideas, they learn to organize their thinking and reflect on concrete representations (Florian and Dean 2001). The activities offered in the lessons engage students in building conceptual understanding while giving the practice necessary for procedural proficiency in calculator use.

In the **Using the Calculator** activities, students move toward abstract understanding. The lessons offer guidance in directing the students to practice using the calculator and improving their skill levels. Graphing calculators facilitate improvement in procedural fluency, the ability to compute, calculate, and use rules and formulas accurately with speed and confidence (Florian and Dean 2001). The **Applying the Concept** and **Extension Ideas** sections bring the students to the real-life applications and further practice. As students move through each phase of learning, they are exposed to a concept or skill numerous times. Per research, students should have multiple experiences with topics, allowing them to integrate the topics into their knowledge base (Marzano 2003). Overall, the challenging and interesting tasks found in application problems help teachers engage students in learning as they actively apply their knowledge (Seely 2004). As a result, students take ownership of new strategies and greater understanding of the ideas and concepts. Through the lesson extension ideas and the activity sheets, the students gain ample opportunities to practice. Students need to have extra time to process concepts and look at problems in different ways (Sutton and Krueger 2002).

Many teachers dread calculator use because of the classroom management issue; however, with proper use, calculators allow teachers to spend more time developing mathematical understanding, reasoning, number sense, and application (Waits and Pomerantz 1997). Therefore, these lessons help teachers respond to that concern by including an introduction with easy-to-follow tips for differentiating the lessons, grouping students, using manipulatives in the lessons, managing the calculators in the classroom, planning the integration of these lessons with standards-based curriculum, and using the graphing calculators in activity centers. The skills reinforced throughout *TI Graphing Calculator Strategies, Algebra* teach multiple representations of mathematical concepts so that students thrive in the mathematic classroom.

The No Child Left Behind (NCLB) legislation mandates that all states adopt academic standards that identify the skills students will learn in kindergarten through grade 12. While many states had already adopted academic standards prior to NCLB, the legislation set requirements to ensure that the standards were detailed and comprehensive.

Correlation to Standards

Standards are designed to focus instruction and guide adoption of curricula. Standards are statements that describe the criteria necessary for students to meet specific academic goals. They define the knowledge, skills, and content students should acquire at each level. Standards are also used to develop standardized tests to evaluate students' academic progress.

In many states today, teachers are required to demonstrate how their lessons meet state standards. State standards are used in the development of Shell Education products, so educators can be assured that they meet the academic requirements of each state.

How to Find Your State Correlations

Shell Education is committed to producing educational materials that are research and standards based. In this effort, all products are correlated to the academic standards of all 50 states, the District of Columbia, and the Department of Defense Dependent Schools. A correlation report customized for your state can be printed directly from the following website: **http://www.shelleducation.com**. If you require assistance in printing correlation reports, please contact Customer Service at 1-800-877-3450.

McREL Compendium

Shell Education uses the Mid-continent Research for Education and Learning (McREL) Compendium to create standards correlations. Each year, McREL analyzes state standards and revises the compendium. By following this procedure, they are able to produce a general compilation of national standards.

Each graphing calculator strategy used in this book is based on one or more of the McREL content standards. The chart on the following pages shows the McREL standards that correlate to each lesson used in the book. To see a state-specific correlation, visit the Shell Education website at **http://www.shelleducation.com**.

Correlation to NCTM Standards

NCTM Standard Grades 9–12	Lesson Title and Page Number
Students will understand the meaning of equivalent forms of expressions, equations, inequalities, and relations.	*Understanding Like Terms* (p. 31); *Conceptualizing Absolute Value* (p. 107); *Solving Absolute Value Equations and Inequalities* (p. 115)
Students will understand and compare the properties of classes of functions, including exponential, polynomial, rational, logarithmic, and periodic functions.	*Combining Like Terms* (p. 40); *Examining Exponential Growth* (p. 194)
Students will develop a deeper understanding of very large and very small numbers and of various representations of them.	*Investigating Direct Variation* (p. 49); *Investigating Roots & Fractional Exponents* (p. 151)
Students will use symbolic algebra to represent and explain mathematical relationships.	*Using Graphs & Tables to Solve Linear Equations* (p. 57)
Students will write equivalent forms of equations, inequalities, and systems of equations and solve them with fluency—mentally or with paper and pencil in simple cases and using technology in all cases.	*Using CALC to Solve Linear Equations* (p. 66); *Solving One-Variable Inequalities* (p. 98); *Exploring Factors, Zeros & Roots* (p. 170); *Determining Number of Quadratic Solutions* (p. 184)
Students will analyze functions of one variable by investigating rates of change, intercepts, zeros, asymptotes, and local and global behavior.	*Analyzing Constant Change & Straightness* (p. 75); *Exploring Slope as a Constant Rate of Change* (p. 82); *Constructing Slope-Intercept Form* (p. 89); *Applying Linear Transformations* (p. 200)

Correlation to NCTM Standards *(cont.)*

NCTM Standard Grades 9–12	Lesson Title and Page Number
Students will interpret representations of functions of two variables.	*Adding & Subtracting to Solve Systems of Equations* (p. 125); *Substituting to Solve Systems of Equations* (p. 132); *Using Inverse Matrices to Solve Systems of Equations* (p. 139)
Students will understand vectors and matrices as systems that have some of the properties of the real-number system.	*Using Inverse Matrices to Solve Systems of Equations* (p. 139)
Students will compare and contrast the properties of numbers and number systems, including the rational and real numbers, and understand complex numbers as solutions to quadratic equations that do not have real solutions.	*Investigating Roots & Fractional Exponents* (p. 151); *Completing the Square* (p. 160); *Determining Number of Quadratic Solutions* (p. 184)

How to Use This Book

TI Graphing Calculator Strategies, Algebra was created to provide teachers with strategies for integrating the TI Graphing Calculator into their instruction for common Algebra I concepts. The lessons are designed to move students from the concrete through the abstract to real-life application, while developing students' graphing calculator skills and promoting their understanding of mathematical concepts.

The table below outlines the major components and purposes for each lesson.

Lesson Components
Lesson Description • Includes two objectives: the first is a mathematics standard and the second is a description of the concepts students will learn
Materials • Lists the activity sheets and templates included with each lesson • Lists additional resources needed, such as manipulatives and the family of TI Graphing Calculators
Explaining the Concept • Concrete instructional methods for promoting students' understanding of math concepts • Often incorporates manipulatives or graphing calculator technology
Using the Calculator • Step-by-step instructions related to the concepts in the lesson • Keystrokes and screen shots provide visual support • Often integrated with the Explaining the Concept section to promote student understanding through graphing calculator use

How to Use This Book *(cont.)*

Lesson Components *(cont.)*

Applying the Concept
- Instructional strategies to promote real-life problem solving and higher-level thinking
- Engaging activities designed around secondary students' interests

Extension Ideas
- Additional lesson ideas for practicing concepts and skills
- Can be used to review, extend, and challenge students' thinking

Activity Sheets
- Teacher- and student-friendly, with easy-to-follow directions
- Often requires students to explain their problem solving strategies and mathematical thinking

---

Icon Guide

To help identify the major instructional parts of each lesson, a corresponding icon has been placed in the margin. In some lessons, these four major instructional phases are independent; in others they are combined.

 Explaining the Concept   Using the Calculator

 Applying the Concept   Extension Ideas

How to Use This Book *(cont.)*

Integrating This Resource into Your Mathematics Curriculum

When planning instruction with this resource, it is important to look ahead at your instructional time line and daily lesson plans to see where *TI Graphing Calculator Strategies, Algebra* can best be integrated into your curriculum. As with most lessons that we teach, the majority of the planning takes place before the students arrive.

The title of each lesson describes the concept taught with the graphing calculator strategies. Preview the lesson titles to find a lesson that correlates with the objective listed in your time line. The **Instructional Time Line** template (page 15) is provided to help integrate this resource into long-range planning.

Implementing the Lessons

After integrating this resource into your instructional time line, use the steps below to help you implement the lessons. The **Instructional Plan** template (page 16) is provided to help determine the resources and lessons to be used for the instructional phases: Explaining the Concept, Using the Calculator, Applying the Concept, Assessments, and Differentiation.

1. Familiarize yourself with the lesson plan. Make sure you have all the materials needed for the lesson.

2. Determine how you want to pace the selected lesson. Each of the lesson parts or instructional phases are mini-lessons that can be taught independently or together, depending on the amount of instructional time and the students' needs.

   - For example, you may choose to use the Explaining the Concept section in place of the lesson taught in the textbook or use the Using the Calculator and the Applying the Concept sections to supplement the textbook.

   - The lesson parts can be taught each day for two or three days, or the lesson can be modified and all three parts can be taught in the course of a 50- or 90-minute instructional block.

3. Solve the problems before class to become familiar with the features on the TI Graphing Calculator, as well as with the math concepts presented.

4. Because space is limited in lesson plan books, use a three-ring binder or a computer folder to keep detailed plans and activities for a specific concept together.

How to Use This Book *(cont.)*

Directions: In the first column, record the date or the days. In the second column, record the standards and/or objectives to be taught on that day. In the third and fourth columns, write the lesson resources to be used to teach that standard and the specific page numbers. In the fifth column, include any adaptations or notes regarding the lesson resources.

Instructional Time Line				
Date	**Standards/ Objectives**	**Lesson Resources, e.g., *Graphing Calculator Strategies*, textbook, etc.**	**Pages**	**Adaptations or Notes**

How to Use This Book *(cont.)*

Directions: Write the date(s) of the lesson in the first column. Write the standards and/or objectives to be taught in the second column. In the remaining columns, write the lesson resources and page numbers to be used for each phase of instruction, as well as any notes and plans for modifying the lessons or differentiating instruction.

Instructional Plan

Date	Standards/Objectives	Lesson Resources Per Instructional Phase				
		Explaining the Concept	Using the Calculator	Applying the Concept	Assessments	Adaptations/ Differentiation
		Pgs.	Pgs.	Pgs.	Pgs.	
		Pgs.	Pgs.	Pgs.	Pgs.	
		Pgs.	Pgs.	Pgs.	Pgs.	
		Pgs.	Pgs.	Pgs.	Pgs.	
		Pgs.	Pgs.	Pgs.	Pgs.	

#50024—*Graphing Calculator Strategies, Algebra* © *Shell Education*

How to Use This Book *(cont.)*

Differentiating Instruction

Students in today's classrooms have a diverse range of ability levels and needs. A teacher is expected to plan and implement instruction to accommodate English-Language Learners (ELL), gifted students, on-level, below-level, and above-level students. The lessons in this resource can be differentiated by their content (what is taught), process (how it is taught), and product (what is created). Below are some strategies that can be used to adapt the lessons in this resource to meet most students' needs. This is not an all-inclusive list and many of the strategies are interchangeable. It is important to implement strategies based on students' learning styles, readiness, and interests.

ELL/ Below-Level	On-Level	Above-Level/ Gifted
• Reduce the number of problems in a set. • Write hints or strategies by specific problems. • Simplify the text on activity sheets. • Create *PowerPoint*™ presentations of lessons and have students use them as a review or reference. • Have students take notes. • Use visual aids and actions to represent concepts and steps of a process. • Act out problems. • Model skills and problems in a step-by-step manner. • Use manipulatives to explain concepts and allow students to use them to complete assignments. • Have students work in homogenous or heterogenous groups. • Have students draw pictures of how they solved the problems.	• Have students take notes. • Have students assist below-level students. • Use activities centered around students' interests. • Have students generate data. • Engage students using *PowerPoint*™, games, and applets. • Have students work in homogenous or heterogenous groups. • Have students write explanations for how they solved the problems. • Use the Extension Ideas to review concepts or skills.	• Have students create how-to guides for functions on the graphing calculator. • Have students use multimedia, such as the TI-SmartView™ or *PowerPoint*™ to present how they solved the problems and/or used the graphing calculator. • Have students work in homogenous groups. • In addition to, or in place of an activity sheet, assign the Extension Ideas. • Have students take on the role of teacher or mentor. • Have students create games for practicing concepts and skills.

How to Use This Book *(cont.)*

Grouping Students

Recommendations for cooperative groups and independent work are given throughout the lessons in this resource. The table below lists the different types of groups, a description of each, and management tips for working with each.

Group Type	Description of Group	Management Tips
Heterogeneous Cooperative Groups	Three to six students with varied ability levels	Give each student a role that suits his or her strengths. Give each group a sheet with directions for the task and a description of each role in completing that task.
Homogeneous Cooperative Groups	Three to six students with similar ability levels	Give each student an equal role in the task by having each student take the lead in a different part or problem of each assignment.
Paired Learning	Two to three students with similar abilities or mixed abilities	When using manipulatives, have students sit side-by-side and give students an opportunity to manipulate the materials.
Independent Work	Students work individually to develop confidence in their abilities.	Closely monitor students' work to correct any misconceptions. This will help students retain the information. This is also a good time to work one-on-one with struggling students or gifted students.

Using Manipulatives

Many of the manipulatives needed for the lessons are templates located in Appendix C of this resource. Below are some tips for using manipulatives in the classroom.

- Use resealable bags or plastic bins to group the manipulatives together. Label manipulatives and place them on a shelf.
- If manipulatives are used for whole-group instruction, have at least one set of manipulatives for each student or for each pair of students. Create a transparency set of manipulatives for modeling on the overhead.
- Use labeled, colored pocket folders to keep activities with multiple components together. Store folders in cardboard storage boxes or sturdy plastic containers.
- Laminate games or instructions on how to use manipulatives to preserve them for multiple uses. Display charts and instructions on a bulletin board in the classroom.

Utilizing and Managing Graphing Calculators

Every minute of class time is valuable. To ensure that adequate time is spent on the lesson and on the usage of the graphing calculator, implement the steps below in your planning.

Methods for Teaching Graphing Calculator Skills

Unlike the four-function calculator, the TI Graphing Calculator has many keyboard zones that will be used to complete the activities in this resource. To help students feel comfortable using the TI Graphing Calculator, follow the steps below before starting a lesson.

1. Demonstrate the most basic graphing calculator skills that students must know to be successful during the **Using the Calculator** section.

2. To teach a skill, have students locate the keys and functions on the calculator and familiarize students with the menus and screens these keys and functions access.

3. If multiple steps are needed to complete the activity, list the steps, on the board, or on the overhead for the students to use as a reference while working. Or use a projector to display the PDF versions of the Using the Calculator sections, which can be printed from the **Teacher Resource CD**.

4. Ask students who are familiar and comfortable using the graphing calculator to assist others. Let the other students know who those graphing calculator mentors are.

5. Allow time to address any questions the students may have after each step or before continuing on to the next part of the lesson.

Storing and Assigning Calculators

- Before using the graphing calculators with students, number each calculator by using a permanent marker or label.

- Assign each student, or pair of students, a calculator number. Since the students will be using the same calculator every time they are distributed, it will help keep track of any graphing calculators that may be damaged or lost.

- Store the calculators in a plastic shoebox or an over-the-door shoe rack. Number the pockets on the shoe rack with the same numbers as the graphing calculators.

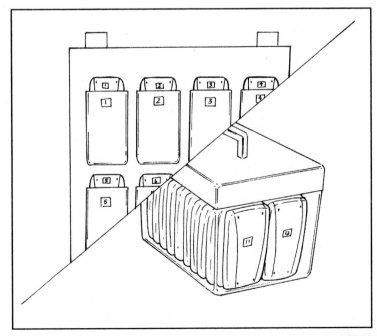

Utilizing and Managing Graphing Calculators *(cont.)*

Distributing Graphing Calculators

To distribute the calculators, consider at which point during the class period the students will need to use them.

- If the students will need the graphing calculators at the beginning of the class period, write "Get your calculator" on the chalkboard or overhead.
- If the calculators are stored in the plastic container, make sure they are in numerical order. This will help students find their calculators faster.
- If the calculators are stored in an over-the-door shoe rack, a note to take a calculator can be placed on the door. This way, the students can grab their calculators as they are walking into the classroom.
- If the calculators will not be used until later in the class period, have the students retrieve their calculators by rows.
- Once the students have their calculators, use the **Check-Off List** (page 21) to keep track of which calculators have been used during that day or class period.

Checking for Damage and Returning Calculators

After distributing the calculators, have students check their calculators for any damage.

- If a calculator is damaged, complete the **Damage Report** (page 22).
- When returning the calculators, have students return their calculators by rows.
- If the calculators are stored in a plastic shoebox, have them put the graphing calculators back in numerical order.
- If the calculators are stored in an over-the-door shoe rack, have the students place them in the correct pockets.
- DO NOT forget to count the calculators before students leave.

Utilizing and Managing Graphing Calculators *(cont.)*

Check-Off List

Student Name	Calculator Number	DATE					

Utilizing and Managing Graphing Calculators *(cont.)*

Damage Report				
Date	Calculator Number	Class Period	Damage	Reported By

Utilizing and Managing Graphing Calculators *(cont.)*

Facilitating a Calculator Center

If only a few calculators are available, create a calculator center in the back of the classroom. One suggested classroom layout is shown below. To prevent students from being distracted and to allow the teacher to work with the students in the center while monitoring the other students, have students sit in the calculator center with their backs toward the other students. Use the **Calculator Center Rotation Schedule** below to keep track of which students have been to the center. While working with the students in the center, provide the other students with independent work. Use the **Check-Off List** (page 21) to keep track of which students used the calculators.

Classroom Layout

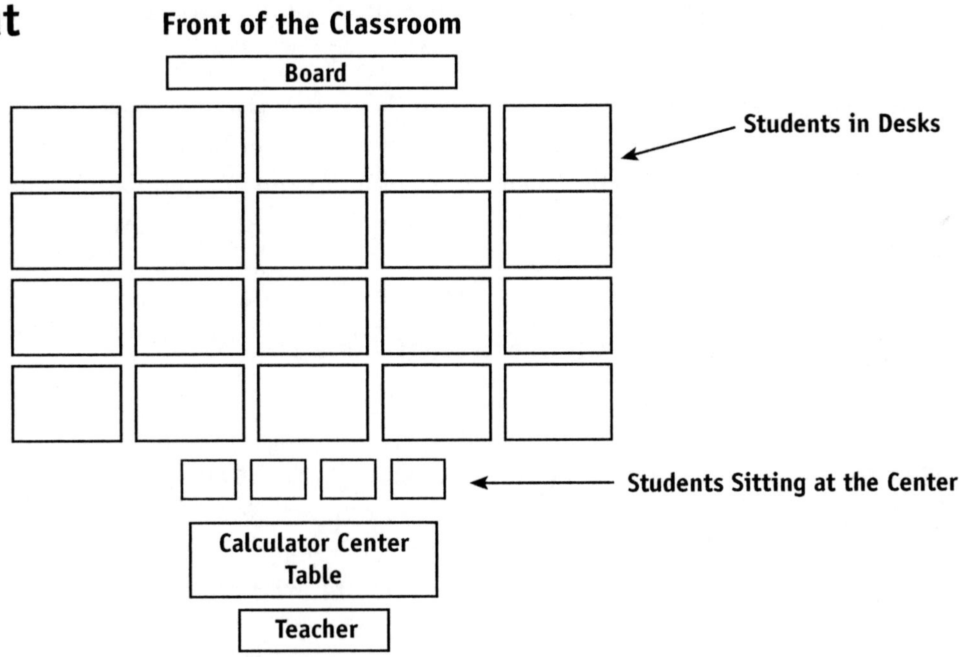

Front of the Classroom

Board

→ **Students in Desks**

← **Students Sitting at the Center**

Calculator Center
Table

Teacher

Calculator Center Rotation Schedule

Days of the Week & Date	Monday	Tuesday	Wednesday	Thursday	Friday
Group Names					
Students					

Assessment

For each lesson, activity sheets are provided that can be used to assess the students' knowledge of the concept. These activities could be considered practice, in which students' progress and understanding of the concept is monitored through an in-class assignment or homework. Or, they can be assigned as a formal assessment. The activity sheets involving real-life application or problem solving can be used as a formally graded activity or assessment.

Completion Grades

To give a completion grade for an activity, have students exchange papers. Review the problems together. Model problems on the overhead or have students model the problems. Have students count the number of problems completed. Then use the **Completion Grades Template** (page 25) to record students' scores.

Write students' names above each column on the **Completion Grades Template**. Write the assignment title in the first column. Record students' scores as a fraction of the number of problems completed over the number of problems assigned. At the end of the grading period, add the number of problems completed for each student to the number of problems assigned. Divide the fraction to calculate a numerical grade.

Using a Point System for Formal Grades

When grading activities that serve as an assessment, it is best to grade them yourself. This provides you with an opportunity to analyze students' performances, evaluate students' errors, and reflect on how instruction may have influenced their performance. It also prevents student error in grading. Depending on a school's grading procedures, assessments can be graded with a fraction similar to completion grades. Determine the number of points each problem is worth. You may want to assign two or more points for each problem, if students are expected to show work or explain how they solved a problem. One point is awarded for the correct answer; the other points are for student's work and/or written explanations. Write a fraction of the number of points a student earned out of the total number of points possible. Record these grades as fractions or convert them to percentages. Then enter them into your grade book or an online grading system.

Grading with a Rubric

A rubric is an alternative way to grade those activities or problems that involve multiple steps or tasks. It allows both the student and teacher to analyze a student's performance for the objectives of the task or assignment by giving the student a categorical score for each component. For example, if the students had the task of solving a problem and explaining how they solved it, a rubric would allow the teacher to identify in which subtasks students excelled or could improve. The problem may be correct, but the explanation may be missing steps needed to solve the problem. The **General Rubric** (page 26) and the **Create Your Own Rubric** (page 27) can be adapted for various types of activities. By using an all-purpose rubric, students can also be individually assessed on specific skills and objectives.

Assessment *(cont.)*

Completion Grades

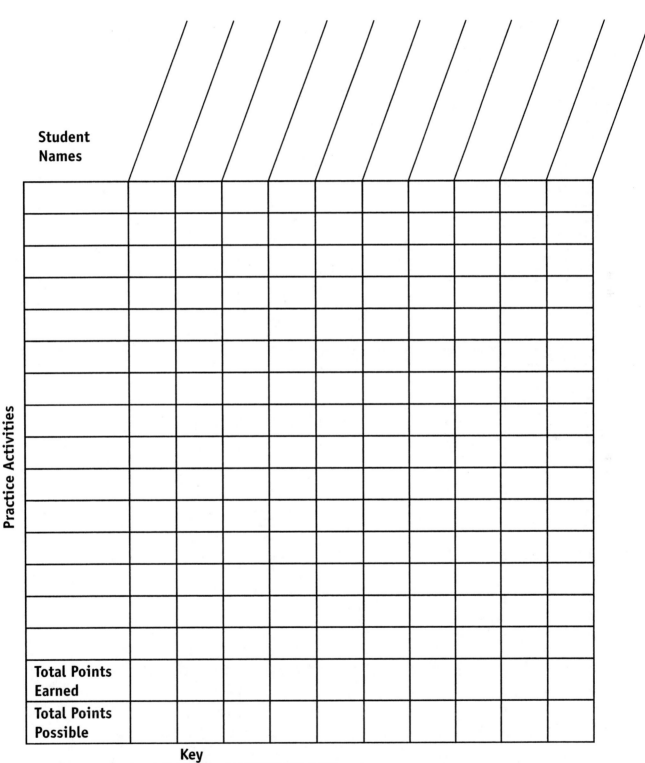

Student Names

Practice Activities

Total Points Earned									
Total Points Possible									

Key

Record Fractions for:
Number of Problems Completed
Number of Possible Problems

Assessment *(cont.)*

General Rubric

Directions: This rubric includes general criteria for grading multistep assignments that involve written explanations to questions. In each of the Level columns, specify each criterion by explaining how it relates to the activity and the levels of performance that can be achieved. Give the rubric to students for self-evaluation and peer evaluation. To evaluate an activity, circle a level of performance for each criterion and assign a number of points. Total the points and record them in one of the last three columns.

Criteria	Level I (0–4 points)	Level II (5–8 points)	Level III (9–10 points)	Self-Score	Peer Score	Teacher Score
Steps in the activity have been completed. Question(s) have been answered.						
Calculations are shown and/or explained.						
Responses relate to the questions being asked.						
Ideas are supported with logical reasoning and/or evidence.						

Assessment *(cont.)*

Directions: Write the criteria of the assignment in the first column. Then for each criterion, fill in the level of performance students may achieve. Give the rubric to the students for self-evaluation and peer evaluation. To evaluate an activity, circle a level of achievement for each criterion and then assign a number of points. Total the points and record them in one of the last three columns.

Create Your Own Rubric

Criteria	Level I (0–4 points)	Level II (5–8 points)	Level III (9–10 points)	Self-Score	Peer Score	Teacher Score

Notes

Unit 1

Understanding Like Terms

Unit 1

Objectives

- Students will learn to add, subtract, and evaluate monomials and polynomials.
- Students will apply simplifying and evaluating polynomials to a real world situation.

Materials

- *Variables One* (pages 36–37; unt1.36.pdf)
- *Popcorn Varies Too!* (page 38; unt1.38.pdf)
- *Variables Rock* (page 39; unt1.39.pdf)
- TI-83/84 Plus Family Graphing Calculator or TI–73 Explorer™

Using the Calculator

Step 1 Show students how to use the memory of the calculator by storing 5 for the variable *n*.

- Press [5] and then [STO▸] to store the number.
- Press [ALPHA] and then [LOG] to access the variable *n*.
- Press [ENTER] to execute the command.

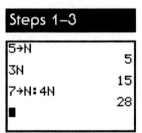

Steps 1–3

```
5→N
                    5
3N
                   15
7→N:4N
                   28
■
```

Step 2 Show students how to use the stored number to evaluate the expression *n*.

- Press [3] to input the value.
- Press [ALPHA] and then [LOG] to input the variable *n*.
- Press [ENTER] to execute the command.

Step 3 Show students how to use concatenation to store a number and complete a computation in one step.

- Repeat **Step 1** above, except store **7** for the variable *n*.
- Then input a colon by pressing [ALPHA] and then [.].
- Input the expression **4*n*** on the same line as the stored variable and the colon.
- Press [ENTER] to execute the command.

Understanding Like Terms *(cont.)*

Unit 1

Using the Calculator *(cont.)*

Step 4

Show students how to recall the last entry and edit it.

- Press **2ND** and then **ENTER**. The last command will be displayed with the cursor flashing at the end of it.

- The flashing cursor means that the line is active and can be edited.

- Use the left arrow to highlight the 7 and change it to a 9.

- Press **ENTER** to evaluate the expression.

Step 4	
5→N	5
3N	15
7→N:4N	28
■→N:4N	

Step 4 *(cont.)*	
	5
3N	15
7→N:4N	28
9→N:4N	36

Explaining the Concept/Using the Calculator

Part I: Understanding Coefficients and Variables

Step 1

Give the students the activity sheet, *Variables One* (pages 36–37).

- You may want to give students two copies of this activity sheet—one to complete during the whole class lesson and the other to complete independently.

- Students will complete **Part I** of the activity sheet in **Steps 2–5**.

Step 2

Explain to students that a variable is a symbol that stands for a number and that the number will vary.

- Instruct students to choose five numbers for the variable *n* and put them on the *Variables One* activity sheet in the *n* column.

- Encourage students to use a variety of numbers for *n* (positive, negative, large, small, etc.).

Step 3

Have students evaluate the expression $n + n + n$ on the graphing calculator.

- Store the first number from the *n* column on the *Variables One* activity sheet for the variable *n* on the calculator. Refer to **Step 2** of the **Using the Calculator** section for how to store a value for a variable.

- Enter a colon and the formula $n + n + n$ on the graphing calculator. Refer to **Steps 3** and **4** of the **Using the Calculator** section (page 31) for how to evaluate expressions using the stored variable.

- Evaluate the expression and record the results in the $n + n + n$ column on the activity sheet *Variables One* (page 36).

Understanding Like Terms *(cont.)*

Unit 1

Step 4

Explaining the Concept/Using the Calculator *(cont.)*

Instruct the students to repeat the procedure above, using the expression 3*n*.

- The students should edit the statement for each of their values for *n* and enter the results in the *n* column on the organizer.

- Discuss with students why the value of *n* + *n* + *n* is dependent upon their choice for *n*.

- Students should record the values in the 3*n* column of the *Variables One* activity sheet (page 36).

- Ask students, "Why are the values in the *n* + *n* + *n* column the same as the values in the 3*n* column?" *Answer: 3n is equivalent to n + n + n.*

- Discuss that although they chose different numbers, everyone had the same values in both of their columns.

- Explain that the 3 is the coefficient in the expression 3*n*. Ask students what the coefficient means in the expression. *Answer: It means three times the value of n.*

Step 5

Ask the students if the expression *n* could have a coefficient.

- Ask students how they could test the coefficient 1 on the calculator.

Step 6

Part II: Understanding Like Terms

Develop students' conceptual understanding of like terms.

- In this activity, students will complete **Parts II–IV** on the *Variables One* activity sheet (pages 36–37).

- Ask the students, "What does the old saying, 'You can't add apples and oranges' mean?"

- Ask the students to propose answers to the question, "What is 5*a* + 3*r* + 2*a* + 4*r*?" Encourage a variety of possibilities.

- Have each student write some *a*'s and some *r*'s on a piece of paper.

- Tell them to write the total number of *a*'s and *r*'s at the top of the paper in the form of coefficient and variable, e.g. 5*a* and 3*r*.

Understanding Like Terms *(cont.)*

Unit 1

Explaining the Concept/Using the Calculator *(cont.)*

Step 7

Each student should partner with a neighbor and count the total number of *a*'s and *r*'s on the two papers. Each pair should write the total in the form shown below.

$$5a + 3r + 7a + 4r = 12a + 7r.$$

Step 7
3→A:7→O:{5A+3O+7 A+4O,12A+7O} {85 85}

- Each pair of students should then partner with another pair to write a sum that represents the total number of *a*'s and *r*'s on all four papers.

- Choose a few groups to write their sums on the board or overhead.

- Check their results by using concatenation as shown in **Steps 1–3** (page 31). The braces allow the calculator to display both results.

- Have the class describe how they can compute the correct answer easily.

Step 8

Discuss the definitions of *variable, coefficient, monomial, polynomial,* and *like terms*.

- Ask the class to propose a rule for adding polynomials.

Step 9

Have each student choose five numbers for *a* and five numbers for *o* and record them on the *Variables One* activity sheet (page 36) or on a separate piece of paper.

- Have them check the results of three of the equations with the procedure used on the previous pages.

Step 10

Have students demonstrate their understanding of like terms by answering the questions in **Part V** on the *Variables One* activity sheet (page 36).

- Have students share their responses with the class.

Applying the Concept

Step 1

Ask students the following questions.

- What is a self-question? *Answer: A question you ask and answer yourself.*

- What are some questions you could ask yourself when solving a math problem? *Answers may vary.*

Understanding Like Terms *(cont.)*

Unit 1

Applying the Concept *(cont.)*

Step 2 Complete the activity sheet, *Popcorn Varies Too!* (page 38) as a whole class.
- Use the activity sheet to model the problem solving strategy of self-questioning to identify the unknown and known information needed to write algebraic expressions and evaluate them on the graphing calculator.
- Together, read the problem on the activity sheet *Popcorn Varies Too!*

Step 3 Have students work with a partner to answer the following self-questions and record the information on the activity sheet.

What do I know?

What are the questions asking?

What other information is needed to answer the question?

What operations are needed to solve the problem?

Step 4 Discuss students' responses to the self-questions.
- Discuss keywords that indicate the operation of multiplication, such as *per, of, by, multiply,* and *product.*

Step 5 Have student volunteers model answering the different questions presented in the problem.
- Have students record the answers on the activity sheet.

Step 6 Have students complete the *Variables Rock* activity sheet (page 39), independently or with a partner.
- Encourage students to use the self-questions to identify the information needed to solve the problems.

Extension Ideas
- Have students write the self-questions they used to complete the activity sheet, *Variables Rock* (page 39).
- Have students create their own problems to simplify like terms, using variables that represent two objects that are opposite.

Name _____

Date _____

Variables One

I. Choose five numbers for the variable *n* and record them in the *n* column in the table below. Evaluate each of the expressions on the graphing calculator by storing the values for *n*.

n	*n + n + n*	*n*

II. There is an old saying, "You can't add apples and oranges." Write an expression with a series of *a*'s and *o*'s on the line below. Count the total number of *a*'s and *r*'s and set it equal to the other side of the expression.

Example: *a + a + a + a + a + r + r + r = 5a + 3r*

_____

- Choose five values for *a* and *o* and evaluate both sides of the expression above on the graphing calculator. Record the values for each side of the expression in the table below.

a	*r*	Left Side	Right Side

Variables One *(cont.)*

III. Partner with a neighbor and write an expression together to represent the sum of a's and r's on the line below.

Example: *5a + 3r + 7a + 4r = 12a + 7r.*

_____

- Choose five values for *a* and *o* and evaluate both sides of the expression on the graphing calculator. Record the values for each side of the expression in the table below.

a	*r*	Left Side	Right Side

IV. You and your partner should find another pair of students to work with. Write an expression to represent the sum of *a*'s and *r*'s the line below.

_____

- Choose five values for *a* and *r* and evaluate both sides of the expression on the graphing calculator. Record the values for each side of the expression in the table below.

a	*r*	Left Side	Right Side

V. Complete the following responses on a separate piece of paper.

- What did you discover about the left and right side of each equation?
- Simplify.   *7a + 2r – 3a – 5r*

Check your answer using the graphing calculator. Then, explain how to combine like terms.

Name _____

Date _____

Popcorn Varies Too!

Directions: Read the problem below.

As pep squad chairperson, you are in charge of ordering popcorn for the football game. Three flavors of popcorn are sold at each game: butter, cheese, and caramel. You order the popcorn from Ready Pop, who makes it and delivers it the day of the game. The cost of the butter popcorn per pound is $5, the cost of cheese popcorn per pound is $6.50, and the cost of caramel popcorn per pound is $7.25.

Write an expression to represent the total cost of ordering all three types of popcorn. Predict the number of pounds of each type of popcorn that should be ordered for the football game. Evaluate the expressions above using your predictions on the graphing calculator. Write an expression to represent the total cost for the order and evaluate it.

Directions: Answer the following self-questions to help you determine the information that is needed to solve the problems above.

a. What do I know?

_____

_____

b. What questions are asked? What tasks do I need to complete?

_____

_____

_____

c. What information is unknown?

_____

_____

d. What operations are needed to solve the problem?

_____

e. Using the information gathered above, answer the questions and complete the tasks given in the problem on the lines below.

_____

_____

_____

Name

Date

Variables Rock

Directions: Read the scenario and answer the questions.

Suppose you own a gravel company and you need to fill a lot of orders. For fine gravel you charge $24 per ton, for medium gravel $21 per ton, and coarse gravel, $18 per ton.

Use the variable f to represent the number of tons of fine gravel, the variable m to represent the number of tons of medium gravel, and the variable c to represent the number of tons of coarse gravel.

a. Complete the table below to find the cost of each order.

Tons of Fine	Cost for Fine	Tons of Medium	Cost for Medium	Tons of Coarse	Cost for Coarse	Total Costs
10		10		10		
20		15		45		
11		75		16		
0		80		10		
f		m		c		

b. Use the expression from the Total Costs column to check the answers using the Store feature on the graphing calculator.

c. Your cost for fine gravel is $22.50 per ton, medium gravel is $18.75 per ton, and coarse gravel is $15.25 per ton. Use the variables f, m, and c to write an expression that represents your cost on an order of gravel. Use your expression to find your cost on the orders above.

d. You find the profit of an order by subtracting your cost from what you charged the customer. Using the variables f, m, and c, write an expression that represents your profit. Use your expression to find your profit on the orders above.

e. By combining like terms, you can write an expression to find your profit by using each variable just once. Write that expression and check your profit again.

f. Which way of finding the profit was more efficient? Explain why.

Combining Like Terms

Unit 1

Lesson Description

- Students will learn to add, subtract, and evaluate monomials and polynomials that include exponents.
- Students will apply combining like terms to a real world situation.

Materials

- *Variables Too!* (pages 44–45; unt1.44.pdf)
- *Like Terms Cards* (pages 46–47; unt1.46.pdf)
- 3-Dimensional Disposable Containers (e.g., a shoe box)
- *Color It* (page 48, unt1.48.pdf)
- **Appendix C:** *Algebra Tiles* (page 215; appnd215.pdf)
- TI-83/84 Plus Family Graphing Calculator and TI-73 Explorer™

Using the Calculator

Step 1   Explain how to access and use the symbols in the Test menu.

- Ask the students to input **2 + 3 = 5** on the graphing calculator. The = is accessed through the Test menu by pressing **2ND** and then **MATH**.
- Press **ENTER** and the calculator should display **1**.
- Have the students enter **2 + 3 = 6**. This time the calculator should display **0**.

Step 2   Have the students enter several problems of their own choosing, using the symbols in the Test menu.

- Ask the class what the **1** and **0** represent.
- Explain that the symbols in the Test menu are Boolean operators, meaning that they will give an answer of True (1) or False (0) to any statement.

Step 3   Explain how to cube a number using the carat symbol.

- Enter a number and then press the caret key **^** followed by a **3**.
- For example to find **5³**, press $\boxed{5}$, $\boxed{^\wedge}$, $\boxed{3}$. Then press **ENTER** to execute the command.

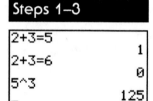

Steps 1–3

```
2+3=5
              1
2+3=6
              0
5^3
            125
■
```

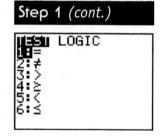

Step 1 (cont.)

```
TEST LOGIC
1:=
2:≠
3:>
4:≥
5:<
6:≤
```

Combining Like Terms *(cont.)*

Unit 1

Using the Calculator *(cont.)*

Step 4 Show students how to cube a number using the ^{3} symbol.

- Press 〔 **5** 〕 to input the base number. Access the command in the Math menu by pressing **MATH**.

- Press 〔 **3** 〕 to select ^{3}, the cube symbol. Press **ENTER** to execute the command.

Step 5 Show students the cube command in the Catalog menu.

- To access **CATALOG**, press **2ND** and then 〔 **0** 〕. Press the up arrow numerous times to locate the ^{3}. Press **ENTER** to select it.

Step 6 Show students how to use concatenation to store a number in memory and complete a computation on the same calculator line and then recall it for editing.

- To store the number 7 for the variable *n*, press 〔 **7** 〕 to enter the value. Then press **STO▸** to access the Store command.

- Press **ALPHA** and then **LOG** to input the variable *n*.

- Complete the computation **4*n*** on the same line by using a colon. Press **ALPHA** and then 〔 **.** 〕 to access the colon.

- Press **ENTER** to execute the command.

Step 7 Show students how to recall the last entry and edit.

- Press **2ND** and then **ENTER**. The previous command will be displayed with the cursor flashing at the end of it. The flashing cursor means that the line is active and can be edited.

- Tell the students to use the left arrow to select the **7** and press 〔 **5** 〕 to change the value.

- Press **ENTER** to execute the command.

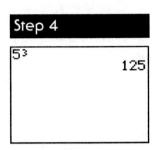

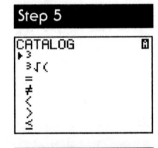

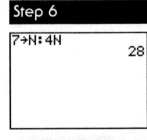

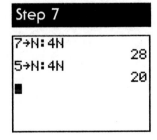

Explaining the Concept / Using the Calculator

Step 1   Give the students the activity sheet, *Variables Too!* (pages 44–45). As a class, investigate like terms using polynomials with exponents.

Step 1
7→M: 2→V: 3MV=MV^3
⁰ -4M: 3→V: 3MV=MV^3
⁰ -4M: 3→V: 3MV=MV^3

- Choose three sets of numbers for *m* and *v*. Enter them in the table for problem **a** on the activity sheet, *Variables Too!*

- Store these values in the memories on the calculator and use concatenation to enter the values and expressions.

- Pose the question, "Is $3mv$ the same as mv^3?" Have students use the Test menu to determine if this is true or false.

- Students should record these answers in the table for problem **b** on the activity sheet, *Variables Too!* Then answer the question for problem **c**.

Step 2   Warn the students about special values and discuss why testing one example is not enough for an investigation.

- Explain that if 0 or 1 is chosen for a variable, the calculator may return a 1.

- A discussion of the special properties of 0 and 1 should illustrate why they are not usually good choices in this kind of work.

Step 3   Ask the students to propose expressions that might be equal to mv^3 and $3mv$.

- Write them in the first and second tables for problem **d** on the activity sheet, *Variables Too!*

- Have students choose values for *m* and *v*, test each expression with the chosen numbers, and write *True* or *False*.

Step 4   Discuss the rules for adding and subtracting simple expressions by combining like terms, using the example below.

$$3a + 2b + 5a - 4b = 8a - 2b$$

- Have students speculate if it is possible to write one expression that is equal to the sum of $3mv + mv^3$. Students should write their answers in the third table in problem **d**.

- Students should test their answers and record if they are true or false.

Step 5   Working with a partner, have students complete problems **e–k** on *Variables Too!*

- Have students present their answers to the class. Or have students record their answers on chart paper and display them around the room.

Applying the Concept

Step 1   Have the class describe like terms with multiple variables and exponents.

Step 2   Distribute the *Like Terms Cards* (pages 46–47) to the class. (Copy the two pages back to back on the same page; there are dots on the back to easily sort the cards into like terms.)

- If there are extra cards, locate them at stations around the room.

- Each student should locate two other cards that have like terms on them.

- Each like term group should compute the sum, check it using the graphing calculator, and write the sum on the board or overhead.

Step 3   Have the students complete the activity sheet, *Color It* (page 48).

- Prior to beginning the activity, show students a shoe box. Discuss the number of faces and edges. Have students identify the dimensions of the box based on those given in the drawing on the *Color It* activity sheet (page 48).

- Cut apart the shoe box to make a one-dimensional net, like the second diagram shown on *Color It*. Discuss the dimensions of the net based on those used in the previous diagram.

- Ask students how to calculate the area of a rectangle.
  Answer: Area = Length x Width

- Ask students how they would find the total surface area of the room using the given values. *Answer: Calculate the areas for the individual rectangles. Then, calculate the sum of the areas.*

Extension Ideas

- Have students collect like terms using Algebra Tiles. An *Algebra Tiles template* is located in Appendix C (page 215). The large squares represent x^2, the rectangles represent x, and the small squares represent 1. The green and blue sides of the tiles are positive, and the red side of the tiles are negative. Use the problem below.

$$2x^2 - x + 5 + x^2 + 2x - 5 = 3x^2 + x$$

- Give small groups disposable containers of simple three-dimensional shapes. Have students cut apart the containers to create nets. Have students draw the container and its net on a separate piece of paper. Using polynomials, students should represent the dimensions of the container and the net. Students should combine the polynomials to find the algebraic surface.

Name _____

Date _____

Variables Too!

Directions: Follow the steps below and answer the questions.

a. Choose three numbers for m and three numbers for v and complete the chart.

b. Answer True or False to the question, "Does $3mv = mv^3$?" for each m and v pair. Record your answers in the table.

	1st number	2nd number	3rd number
m			
v			
$3mv$			
mv^3			
True or False			

c. Does $3mv = mv^3$? (Hint: It must always be true to answer yes.)

_____

d. Choose numbers for m and v. In the Possibility columns, write expressions that you think might be equal to the expression. Evaluate the expressions and write *true* if the value is equal to that of the expression and *false* if it is not.

	m	v	Expression mv^3	Possibility 1	Possibility 2
Value					
True or False					
	m	v	Expression $3mv$	Possibility 1	Possibility 2
Value					
True or False					

Name _____

Date _____

Variables Too! *(cont.)*

Follow the directions on the previous page.

	m	v	Expression $3mv + mv^3$	Possibility 1	Possibility 2
Value					
True or False					

e. Why is it not possible to write $3mv + mv^3$ as one term?

_____

_____

f. Write three terms that are like terms with $3mv$ below.

$3mv$			

g. Add and subtract all the like terms.

_____

_____

h. Choose values for m and v and test your answers. Record your tests below.

_____

_____

i. Write three terms that are like terms with mv^3.

mv^3			

j. Add and subtract all the like terms.

_____

_____

k. Choose values for m and v and test your answers. Record your tests below.

Name _____

Date _____

Like Terms Cards *(Front)*

Directions: Photocopy the cards front and back with those on page 47. Cut them apart. Give each student one card. Each group should locate two other cards with like terms on them. Each like term group should compute the sum and check it on the graphing calculator.

x^2y	$-5x^2y$	$12x^2y$	$8xy$	xy	$-6xy$
$12xy^3$	$-6xy^3$	$10xy^3$	x^2y^2	$11x^2y^2$	$-4x^2y^2$
x^3y^2	$-5x^3y^2$	$2x^3y^2$	$4x^3y^4$	x^3y^4	$-10x^3y^4$
x^3z	$-3x^3z$	$5x^3z$	xz^4	$-2xz^4$	$7xz^4$
x^3z^4	$-6x^3z^4$	$3x^3z^4$	y^3z^2	$6y^3z^2$	$-5y^3z^2$
xy^3z^2	$2xy^3z^2$	$-xy^3z^2$	x^2y^3z	$-8x^2y^3z$	$11x^2y^3z$

Name _____

Date _____

Like Terms Cards *(Back)*

.	.	.	..	..	..
.	.	.	..	..	..
.	.	.	..	..	..
...	...	...	....	.....	.....
.	.	.	..	..	..
...	...	...	....	....	....

Name _____

Date _____

Color It

Directions: You need to paint all the walls, ceiling, and floor of a rectangular room with the dimensions described in terms of *p*, *q*, and *r*. The dimensions are given in feet.

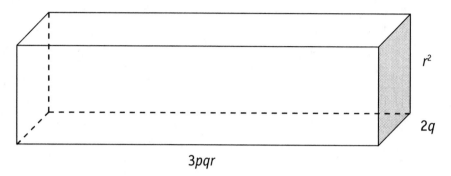

r^2

$2q$

$3pqr$

Directions: Write the dimensions of the flat model of the room along each side. Write the area of each section inside the diagram.

Directions: Write the total area of the surfaces in simplest form (with all like terms combined). Use the memory on your calculator to find the total area to be painted if *p*, *q*, and *r* have the values below.

The total surface area to be painted is _____

p	*q*	*r*	**Area**
3.1	4.5	2.2	
2.6	5.1	1.6	
5	2.5	1.4	

Investigating Direct Variation

Unit 1

Lesson Description

- Students will solve problems involving direct variation and identify relationships among variables through the use of a spreadsheet.
- Students will apply direct variation, proportion, and percent to real-life scenarios.

Materials

- *It's Direct!* (pages 55–56; unt1.55.pdf)
- TI-83/84 Plus Family Graphing Calculator or TI-73 Explorer™

Using the Calculator

Step 1 Show students how to use the SetUp editor.

- Press **STAT** and then **5** to access the **SetUp Editor**.
- Press **ENTER**. The word **Done** will appear on the screen indicating that the list has been inserted.

Step 2 Show students how to access the Stat List editor and clear the lists.

- Press **STAT** and then **1** to access the Stat List editor.
- To clear a list, use the up arrow to highlight the list name.
- Press **CLEAR** and then **ENTER**.
- Repeat the steps to clear lists **L1** through **L6**.

Step 3 Model how to enter data in a list.

- Have students input **{1, 2, 3, 4, 5, 6}** into **L1** by placing the cursor under **L1** and pressing the number followed by **ENTER**, e.g. **1**, **ENTER**, **2**, **ENTER**, etc.

Step 1

```
EDIT CALC TESTS
1:Edit…
2:SortA(
3:SortD(
4:ClrList
5▯SetUpEditor
```

Step 1 *(cont.)*

```
SetUpEditor
            Done
▮
```

Step 2

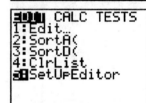

Step 3

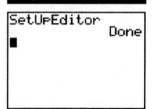

Investigating Direct Variation *(cont.)*

Unit 1

Using the Calculator *(cont.)*

Step 4

Show students how to perform operations on the list, placing the results in **L2**.

- Highlight **L2** and then press **ENTER**.

- When the cursor flashes on the edit row at the bottom of the screen, input the expression **3L1**. Press (**3**), followed by **2ND** and then (**1**) to access **L1**.

- Press **ENTER** to evaluate the expression for the values given in **L1**.

Special Note: By entering a formula this way, the lists are not interactive. Changing **L1** will not change **L2**. An interactive spreadsheet method will be introduced later.

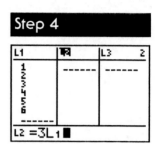

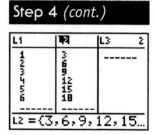

Explaining the Concept/Using the Calculator

Step 1

Ask students, "What is direct variation?"
Answer: Two variable quantities that always have a constant ratio

- If students are unsure of the meaning, dissect the vocabulary term by looking at general meanings of each word.

- Explain to students that this is an example of direct variation because every number in List 1 is multiplied by the same number to create a constant proportion between the values in **L1** and **L2**.

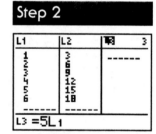

Step 2

Have students define **L3**, by inputting the list formula **5L1**.

- Press the up arrow to highlight **L3** and press **ENTER**.

- Press (**5**), **2ND**, and then (**1**) to enter the list formula next to **L3 =**.

- Press **ENTER** to execute the command.

- Ask students if this is also an example of direct variation, and if so, why?

*Answer: As the values in **L1** increase, so do the values in **L3** by a constant ratio.*

Investigating Direct Variation *(cont.)*

Unit 1

Explaining the Concept/Using the Calculator *(cont.)*

Step 3   Model how to set up the calculator to create a scatter plot of the direct variation of data in L1 and L2.

- Before beginning the graph, press **Y=**. Clear any equations by moving the cursor to any equation and pressing **CLEAR**.

- While on the Y= screen, ensure that the stat plots at the top of the screen are not highlighted. If they are highlighted, highlight the plot and press **ENTER** to deselect them.

- Press **MODE** and ensure that the default, (left-hand) settings are highlighted. To change a setting, use the arrows to move to the desired setting and press **ENTER**.

- Check the Format screen by pressing **2ND** and then **ZOOM** to ensure that all the default (left-hand) settings are selected.

Step 4   Show students how to set up a scatter plot using **L1** for the *x*-values and **L2** for the *y*-values.

- Press **2ND** and then **Y=** to access the Stat Plot editor. Press **1** to select **Plot1**.

- Select the following settings by highlighting each and pressing **ENTER**. Turn **On** Plot1. By **Type:** select the first icon, which represents a scatter plot.

- By **Xlist**, press **2ND** followed by **1** to input **L1**. By **Ylist**, press **2ND** followed by **2** to input **L2**. By **Mark**, select the 1st icon. The first icon by mark means that the calculator will show small squares for each data point.

Step 3

Step 3 *(cont.)*

Step 3 *(cont.)*

Step 4

Step 4 *(cont.)*

Investigating Direct Variation *(cont.)*

Unit 1

Explaining the Concept/Using the Calculator *(cont.)*

Step 5

Model how to set up an accommodating window to display the scatter plot.

- Press **window**. Enter the values shown in the screen shot.

- Discuss the choices for Xmin, Xmax, Ymin, and Ymax. Explain that Xscl and Yscl indicates the spaces between tick marks. Xres is the resolution of the graph, which should be set at 1.

Special Note: The *x*-axis is 94 pixels across. When the calculator divides the pixels evenly into negative and positive integers, each pixel represents one tick mark. Therefore, *x*-values can go from –47 to 47. The *y*-axis has 62 pixels vertically and stretches from –31 to 31. Twenty or fewer tick marks make for nice axes.

Step 6

Have students graph the scatter plot.

- Press **graph**. Ask students to describe the pattern of the points. *Answer: The points lie on a line that goes through the origin.*

- Ask students why the line should go through the origin if the second list is in direct variation with the first.

Step 7

Have students set up Plot 2.

- Press **2ND**, **Y=** and then **2** to access **Plot2**.
- Input **L1** for the **Xlist** and **L3** for the **Ylist**.
- Select the + mark for this scatter plot.
- Then press **graph**. Ask students to describe this graph.

Step 8

Exemplify how a relation that exhibits direct variation is in the form $y = kx$.

- Press **Y=**. Input **Y₁ = 3x** and **Y₂ = 5x**. Press **x,t,θ,n** to access *x*.

- Press **graph**. A screenshot of the graph is on page 53.

- Ask students to describe the relationship between the lines and the stat plots.

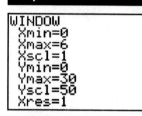

Step 5

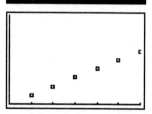

Step 6 & 7

Step 7 *(cont.)*

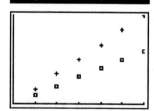

Step 7 *(cont.)*

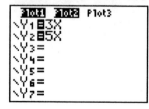

Step 8

Explaining the Concept/Using the Calculator *(cont.)*

Step 9

Make the lists interactive and check more points.

- To make the lists interactive, reenter the formulas for **L2** and **L3** with the formulas in quotation marks by pressing **ALPHA** and then **+** at the beginning and end of the formula.

Step 10

Have the students add more values to L1.

- Ask them what happened to L2 and L3? *Answer: They will update automatically.*

- Have students choose new windows to include all of their points.

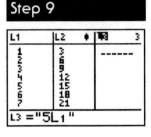

Applying the Concept

Step 1

Discuss how percents and ratios are applications of direct variation.

- Explain that a relationship in the form $y = kx$ is an example of direct variation, but it is also a proportion. Model this, using the problem below.

$$y = \frac{2}{3}x$$

- Have students divide each side by x and get the proportion.

$$y = \frac{2}{3}x$$

$$\frac{y}{x} = \frac{2}{3}$$

- Point out that the statement $y = \frac{2}{3}(18)$ is equivalent to the proportion, $\frac{y}{18} = \frac{2}{3}$.

- This proportion can be solved using cross products.

$$3y = 36$$
$$y = 12$$

Investigating Direct Variation *(cont.)*

Unit 1

Applying the Concept *(cont.)*

Step 2 Have students write equivalent statements of the proportion y/x = 4/5 in both forms.

- Ask students what they should do before they can rewrite the statement. *Answer: Begin by solving for y.*

$$5y = 4x$$

$$y = \frac{4x}{5}$$

Step 3 Propose the statement "*y* is 45% of *x*."

- Have the students rewrite it in the form *y* = 45*x*/100, and ask students why the problem is an example of direct variation.

- Ask the students to rewrite this as the proportion $\frac{y}{x} = \frac{45}{100}$.

Step 4 Have the students work in small groups to rewrite the questions "What is 60% of 90?" and "80 is 40% of what?" as proportions.

- Point out that whatever follows the word "of" is called the *base* and is used in place of the *x* in the proportion. Using the base as the denominator on the left is an easy way to set up a proportion for solving any percent problems.

Step 5 Have students complete the activity sheet, *It's Direct!* (page 55).

Extension Ideas

- Have students work in small groups to find examples of direct variation in magazine and newspaper articles. Have them create a collage, book, poster, or *PowerPoint*™ presentation of their examples. For each example, have students describe the relationship.

- Have students investigate scenarios that represent the inverse variation, $y = \frac{k}{x}$.

Name _____

Date _____

It's Direct!

Directions: Tips in a restaurant are a direct relationship to the cost of the bill. Read the scenario below and then follow the steps to complete the tables.

Devon just started working as a waiter at a local restaurant where many of his friends and classmates hang out. Devon's wage is $2.33 per hour, plus tips. Devon's salary is dependent on how much money he makes from tips, but Devon's friends don't know how to calculate tax or tip and as a result often give him less than 15% of the total check. Devon has decided to create the following tables and graphs to help his friends calculate tax and tip for common amounts.

a. Enter list formulas into the Stat List editor to calculate the values for the table below. Use quotation marks so that they can be edited and updated. Input the values for *n* in **L1**, 15% of *n* in **L2**, *n* + 15% of *n* in **L3**, and 115% of *n* in **L4**. On the Mode menu, arrow down to FLOAT and select 2 decimal places.

b. Write the list formulas entered below each column. In the second and fourth column, write the formulas in the form $y = kx$.

c. Record the list data calculated in the table below.

L1 *n*	L2 15% of *n*	L3 *n* + 15% of *n*	L4 115% of *n*
List Formulas			
30			
70			
45			
120			
10			
65			
x			

d. Make two scatter plots of the data, using L1 and L2 for the first plot, and L1 and L4 for the second plot. Then enter formulas for the data in Y₁ and Y₂. Graph the scatter plots and lines together. Draw them in the box.

Name _____

Date _____

It's Direct! *(cont.)*

e. Edit the formulas in your lists to calculate 5.75% tax on purchases. Record the formulas in the table below.

f. Record the list data calculated in the table below.

L1 *n*	L2 5.75% of *n*	L3 *n* + 5.75% of *n*	L4 105.75% of *n*
List Formulas			
30			
70			
45			
120			
10			
65			
x			

g. Adjust the window for your new data, change the formulas in Y_1 and Y_2, and regraph the equations.

h. Suppose a plumber charges $50 for a house call and $18 per hour while he is working. Write a formula for his charges and record it on the line below.

_____

i. Input the formula in the Y= screen. Then enter the following window settings *X* [−2, 8] and *Y* [0, 150]. Create a graph and draw it in the box on the right.

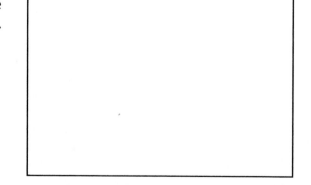

j. How does the graph show that this is not an example of direct variation? How is the equation different from direct variation?

_____

_____

Using Graphs & Tables to Solve Linear Equations

Unit 1

Lesson Description

- Students will write and solve one-step linear equations with one variable and interpret the solution of the equation.
- Students will verify the reasonableness of the results.

Materials

- *Show Me* (pages 63–64; unt1.63.pdf)
- *Ups and Downs* (page 65; unt1.65.pdf)
- TI-83/84 Plus Family Graphing Calculator or TI-73 Explorer™

Using the Calculator

Step 1 Have the students solve the following equation by graphing it on the calculator.

$$x - 1 = 2$$

- Tell students they will use the Trace feature to find the intersection on the graph and they will use the Table feature to verify the intersection.
- Explain that they will create two graphs, one for each side of the equation.

Step 2 Show students how to prepare the calculator to graph equations.

- Select **MODE** and choose the default settings shown in the screen shot, by using the arrow keys to highlight each and then pressing **ENTER**.

- Access **FORMAT** by pressing **2ND** followed by **ZOOM**. Using the same method, select the default settings by highlighting all the selections on the left and pressing **ENTER** after each.

Step 3 Show students how to enter $y = x - 1$ and $y = 2$ into the equation editor and graph the lines in a decimal window.

- Press **Y=**. If any of the plots at the top of the screen are highlighted, press **ENTER** to turn them off.
- Enter $x - 1$ into Y_1. Enter 2 into Y_2. Use the **X,T,θ,n** key to insert x.

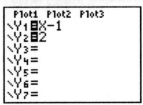

Using Graphs & Tables to Solve Linear Equations *(cont.)*

Unit 1

Using the Calculator *(cont.)*

Step 4 Have students create a ZDecimal window.

- Press **ZOOM** and then **4**.
- Press **WINDOW** to view the values and discuss them.

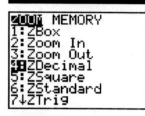

Step 5 Demonstrate how the graph screen displays coordinates.

- Press **GRAPH**. Use the arrows to move around the screen. Point out that the coordinates of each point are displayed at the bottom of the screen.
- Identify the Xmin, Xmax, Ymin, and Ymax values.

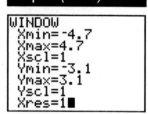

Step 6 Explain how to trace on the graph screen.

- Press **TRACE**. A cursor will appear on one of the lines with the equation of that line at the top of the screen.
- To toggle to the other line, press the up/down arrows.
- To view the points along the graph of an equation, use the right/left arrows.
- Students should notice that the *x*-values increase by 0.1. The *y*-values are determined by the equations.

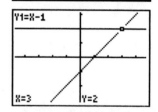

Step 7 Instruct students to find the intersection of the lines.

- Trace to the point where the lines appear to cross.
- Toggle between the lines to see if the same point is displayed on both equations. If so, this is the *x*-value that makes both sides of the equation true. This should be point (3, 2).

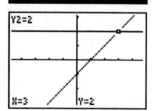

Step 8 Show how to use the Table feature to find the intersection.

- Access **TBLSET** by pressing **2ND** followed by **WINDOW**. Adjust the settings as shown in the screen shot.
- In **TBLSET**, the value for **TblStart** is 0, indicating the *x*-values will begin at 0.
- Ask the students how the ∆Tbl setting affects the *x*-values in the table. *Answer: This is the scale, or increment of the x-values.*

Using Graphs & Tables to Solve Linear Equations *(cont.)*

Unit 1

Using the Calculator *(cont.)*

Step 9

Analyze the values displayed in the table.

- To display the table, access **TABLE** by pressing **2ND** and then **GRAPH**.

- Remind students that they entered $x - 1$ in Y_1 and **2** in Y_2.

- Ask students how the calculator determined the numbers under Y_1 and Y_2.

- Use the up/down arrows to scroll through the table. Move the cursor to the top of a y column to view the equation at the bottom of the screen.

- Have them locate the place where the values in Y_1 and Y_2 are the same. This should occur where $x = 3$.

Step 10

Model how to use the split screen feature to see the table on the left and the graph on the right.

- Press **MODE**. Use the arrows to move to **G-T** in the second to last row, and press **ENTER**.

- Press **GRAPH** to view both the graph and table at the same time.

- Trace to view the highlighted values in the table that correspond to the points on the graph.

Step 11

To obtain one-place decimal values, return to the Decimal window.

- Press **ZOOM** and then select **4: ZDecimal**.

- When you trace to find the solution, the window will automatically adjust.

Step 9

X	Y1	Y2
0	-1	2
1	0	2
2	1	2
3	2	2
4	3	2
5	4	2
6	5	2

X=0

Step 10

Steps 10 & 11 *(cont.)*

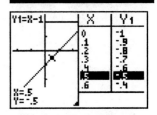

Step 11 *(cont.)*

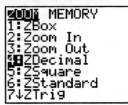

Using Graphs & Tables to Solve Linear Equations *(cont.)*

Unit 1

Explaining the Concept/Using the Calculator

Step 1   Explain the difference between linear equations and equivalent equations.

- Explain that the equations previously graphed were linear equations.

- Explain that to solve linear equations, they should be converted into equivalent equations. Also explain that the equivalent equations have the same solution.

Step 2   Explain that solving a linear equation using algebra involves adding 1 to each side of the equation to create a series of equivalent equations.

$$x - 1 = 2$$
$$x - 1 + 1 = 2 + 1$$
$$x = 3$$

Step 3   Have students enter equivalent equations on the graphing calculator.

- Return to the Equation editor by pressing **Y=**.

- Ask them what two entries they should graph to show the solution of the equation above.

- Enter *x* into **Y₃** and **3** into **Y₄**. (Input *x* by pressing **x,т,ø,n**.)

- Turn **Y₁** and **Y₂** off by using the arrows to move the cursor over the equal sign and pressing **ENTER** to un-highlight them.

Step 4   Together, analyze the values shown on the graph/table split screen.

- Press **window** and change the Ymin and Ymax values to those shown in the screen shot on the right. (This will allow the students to trace "friendly numbers" on the split screen.)

- Press **GRAPH** to see graphs and table values for only those equations entered into **Y₃** and **Y₄**.

- Use the Trace feature to find the point of intersection of these two graphs.

Step 3

```
Plot1 Plot2 Plot3
\Y1=X-1
\Y2=2
\Y3∎X
\Y4∎3
\Y5=
\Y6=
\Y7=
```

Step 4

```
WINDOW
 Xmin=-2.3
 Xmax=2.3
 Xscl=1
 Ymin=-3.1
 Ymax=3.1
 Yscl=1
 Xres=1
```

Step 4 *(cont.)*

Using Graphs & Tables to Solve Linear Equations *(cont.)*

Unit 1

Explaining the Concept/Using the Calculator *(cont.)*

Step 5 Show students how to graph all four equations.

- Press **MODE** and return the calculator to Full Screen by selecting **FULL**.

- Press **Y=** and turn **Y₁** and **Y₂** back on by moving the cursor over the equal signs and pressing **ENTER** to highlight them.

- Press **ZOOM** and then select **4: ZDecimal**.

Step 5

Step 5 *(cont.)*

Step 6 Have students use the Draw feature to identify the point of intersection of all four graphs.

- While on the graphing screen, select **DRAW** by pressing **2ND** and then **PGRM**. Press **4** to select **Vertical**.

- Use the right arrow key to move the vertical line to cross the points of intersection of **Y₁** and **Y₂** and the intersection of **Y₃** and **Y₄**.

- Ask the class what the vertical line shows about the intersections of the pairs of lines.

- Notice that the equations $x - 1 = 2$ and $x = 3$ have the same solution and are equivalent.

Step 5 *(cont.)*

Step 7 Have students solve the equations $x - 3 = 2$ and $x + 2 = -2$ algebraically, by tracing the graphs and viewing the values in the table.

Step 8 Have students complete the activity sheet, *Show Me* (pages 63–64) to practice the relationship between algebraic, graphical, and tabular solutions.

Step 6

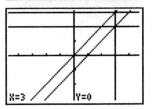

Step 6 *(cont.)*

Using Graphs & Tables to Solve Linear Equations *(cont.)*

Unit 1

Applying the Concept

Step 1 Lead a discussion involving situations where we use the concepts of *more than* and *less than*. Use the following scenario:

Joe ran five miles less than Mike, and Joe ran 7.5 miles.

- Help students represent the scenario with the equation $7.5 = m - 5$.

Step 2 Have students work with a partner to represent the following scenario with a linear equation.

The water temperature must be 82 degrees before Rosa's mother will let her swim. The temperature is going up one degree each day and is currently 75 degrees. How soon will Rosa be able to swim?

- The equation $82 = 75 + d$ represents the above scenario.

Step 3 Have students complete the activity sheet, *Ups and Downs* (page 65).

Extension Ideas

- Have students investigate the difference between functions and linear equations.

- To make the idea of solving a linear equations more concrete, have students construct a balance. Tape half of an index card to each side of a straw. Balance the straw on a pencil. Have students use paper clips to represent the value of the variable.

Name _____

Date _____

Show Me

Directions: Solve each of the equations algebraically, showing all steps. Then, check your answer with a graph and a table. For each, give the equations you enter into the calculator, sketch the graph and the table, and circle the point that shows the solution on both the graph and the table.

a. $x + 2 = -1$

Solution	Equations
	$Y_1 =$ $Y_2 =$

Graph	Table

b. $x - 5 = -2$

Solution	Equations
	$Y_1 =$ $Y_2 =$

Graph	Table

Name _____

Date _____

Show Me *(cont.)*

c. $x + 4 = 3$

Solution	Equations
	$Y_1 =$ $Y_2 =$

Graph	Table

d. $x - 1 = -2$

Solution	Equations
	$Y_1 =$ $Y_2 =$

Graph	Table

Name _____

Date _____

Ups and Downs

Directions: For each of the following problems, write and solve an equation. Even though the answer to the question may be obvious, learning how to write the equation and how to solve it is the focus of this activity. The equation should be either in the form $x + 3 = 7$ or $x - 3 = 7$.

a. Eliza lives 2 miles farther from school than Henry lives. Eliza lives 13 miles from the school. How far from the school does Henry live?

b. Henry's sister is 3 years younger than Eliza. Eliza is 15 years old. How old is Henry's sister?

c. Eliza is saving her earnings from her part-time job to buy a new MP3 player. She has $143 saved, and the MP3 player costs $203. How much more money does she need for her purchase?

d. Henry is 7 inches taller than Eliza. If Henry is 73 inches tall, how tall is Eliza?

e. Eliza's baby sister weighs 4 lbs. less than Henry's baby brother. If Henry's brother weighs 22 lbs., how much does Eliza's sister weigh?

f. Eliza can run a mile in 9 minutes. Henry's time is 1.5 minutes longer. How long does it take Henry to run a mile?

Using CALC to Solve Linear Equations

Unit 1

Lesson Description

- Students will write and solve one-step linear equations with one variable.
- Students will interpret the solution of an equation and verify the reasonableness of the results.

Materials

- *Check It Out!* (pages 71–72; unt1.71.pdf)
- **Appendix C:** Algebra Tiles (page 215; appnd215.pdf)
- TI-83/84 Plus Family Graphing Calculator or TI-73 Explorer™

Using the Calculator

Step 1

Explain how to solve the equation $7x = 8$ on the graphing calculator.

- Tell students that they will graph equations and then use the intersection feature on the **CALC** menu.

- Explain that two graphs will be created. One graph will be of the coefficient and variable, the other will be of the constant.

Step 2

Show students how to prepare the calculator to graph equations.

- Press **MODE** and choose the default settings shown in the screen shot. To change a setting, highlight it and press **ENTER**.

- Access **FORMAT** by pressing **2ND** followed by **ZOOM**. Select the default settings by highlighting all the selections on the left.

Step 3

Show students how to enter $y = 7x$ and $y = 8$ into the equation editor.

- Press **Y=**.

- Enter **7x** into **Y₁** and **8** into **Y₂**. (Press **X,T,Ø,n** to insert **x**.)

- If any of the Plots at the top of the screen are highlighted, move the cursor over them and press **ENTER** to turn them off.

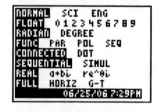

Using CALC to Solve Linear Equations *(cont.)*

Unit 1

Using the Calculator *(cont.)*

Step 4

Create a ZStandard window and discuss the meaning of the window values.

- Press **ZOOM** and then (**6**) to select **ZStandard**. Press **WINDOW** to view the settings.

- Xres controls graphing speed and should be left at 1 Xmin, Xmax, Ymin, and Ymax represent the least and greatest values on the *x*- and *y*-axes.

- Model how to use Xmin, Xmax, Ymin, and Ymax to express the window in the form *X*[–10, 10] and *Y*[–10, 10].

Step 5

Model for students how to use Trace function.

- Press **TRACE**. The cursor will appear on one of the lines with the equation of that line at the top of the screen.

- The coordinates of each point are displayed at the bottom of the screen.

- To toggle to the other line, press the up/down arrows.

- To view the points along the graph of an equation, use the right/left arrows.

- Explain that the *x*-values increase by 0.21276596 at a time because there are 94 pixels across the screen (20, the number of units across the screen, divided by 94 is 0.21276596). The *y*-values are determined by the equations.

Step 6

Find the point of intersection of *y* = 7*x* and *y* = 8.

- Ask the students, "At which point does the graph show the same *x* and *y* values for *y* = 7*x* and *y* = 8?"

- Have students trace along the line *y* = 7*x* until they reach that point exactly.

- Students will find that it is not possible to trace to a point where the *y*-value is exactly 8 for the equation 7*x*.

Step 4

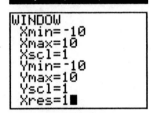

Step 4 *(cont.)*

WINDOW
 Xmin=-10
 Xmax=10
 Xscl=1
 Ymin=-10
 Ymax=10
 Yscl=1
 Xres=1█

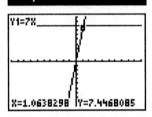

Step 5 & 6

Y1=7X

X=1.0638298   Y=7.4468085

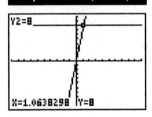

Step 5 & 6 *(cont.)*

Y2=8

X=1.0638298   Y=8

Using CALC to Solve Linear Equations *(cont.)*

Unit 1

Using the Calculator *(cont.)*

Step 7 Tell the students that the calculator has a built-in method of finding the point of intersection.

- Access **CALC** by pressing `2ND` and then `TRACE`.
- On the Calc menu, press `5` to select **intersect**.

Step 8 Answer the prompts on the Graph screen to identify the intersection.

- For the prompt "**First curve?**" press `ENTER` to indicate the first line.
- The cursor will switch to the other line. The prompt "**Second curve?**" will appear. Press `ENTER` to indicate the second line.
- These prompts are necessary when there are more than two equations graphed. In that case, press the up/down arrows to move the cursor to a different graph on that screen and press `ENTER`.
- For the final prompt "**Guess?**" move the cursor close to the point of intersection.
- Press `ENTER` to view the coordinates of the intersection.
- Ask the students which coordinate is the solution to the equation. *Answer: Intersection, (1.1428571, 8).*

Step 9 Model how to check the solution.

- Ask the students how to check if the number they found is a solution to the equation $7x = 8$.
- To show the substitution of the solution for x, return to the Home screen. Choose **QUIT** by pressing `2ND` and then `MODE`.
- Press `X,T,θ,n` and then `ENTER`, entering x will recall the last value used on the graphing screen at the point of intersection.
- To test if the value is a solution, input $7x$ and `ENTER`.
- To see the solution as a fraction, tell them to move to press `X,T,θ,n`, `MATH`, and select **1:▶Frac** and then `ENTER`.
- View the screen shot for this step on page 69.

Step 7

Step 8

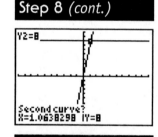

Step 8 *(cont.)*

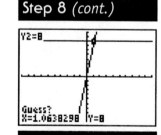

Step 8 *(cont.)*

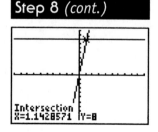

Step 8 *(cont.)*

Using CALC to Solve Linear Equations *(cont.)*

Unit 1

Explaining the Concept/Using the Calculator

Step 1

Ask students to solve the equation $3x = 11$.

- Show students how to divide both sides of the equation by 3 to find the solution.

$$\frac{3x}{3} = \frac{11}{3}$$

$$x = \frac{11}{3} \text{ or } 3\frac{2}{3}$$

Step 2

Have students solve the equation above graphically.

- Press [Y=]. Delete the equations entered by positioning the cursor on each equation and pressing [CLEAR].

- Ask the students which expressions should be entered to find the solution of the equation graphically.

- Enter **3x** into **Y₁** and **11** into **Y₂**. Select [ZOOM] and then **6: Zstandard** to graph the equations.

- View the window values ([WINDOW]) and then return to the Graph screen by pressing [GRAPH].

Step 3

Ask the students why they can only see one line of the graph in the ZStandard window. Discuss how they could change the window to see both lines.

- Create an appropriate window by selecting [WINDOW] and entering a number greater than 11 for **Ymax**.

- Show the windows created by students on the projected graphing calculator.

- Write the window in the form X[Xmin, Xmax] and Y[Ymin,Ymax].

Step 4

Have students find the solution to $3x = 11$ using the intersection feature on the CALC menu.

- Refer to **Steps 7–8** in the **Using the Calculator** section.

- Check the solution and express it as a fraction. Refer to **Step 9** in the **Using the Calculator** section.

Step 9
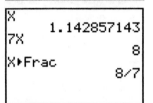

Step 2
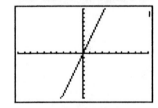

Step 2 (cont.)

Step 3
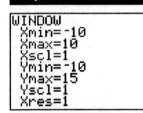

Step 4
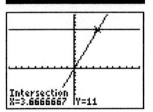

Using CALC to Solve Linear Equations *(cont.)*

Unit 1

Step 5

Step 1

Explaining the Concept/Using the Calculator *(cont.)*

Have the students find the solution of $3x = -35$ graphically.

- Ask the students how to adjust the Ymin to see both lines.

- When the graph still does not display the point of intersection, ask the students how to change the window so that the point of intersection is visible.

- Discuss why changing the window to x[–15, 10] and y[–40, 10] shows the point of intersection.

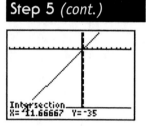

- Have the students identify the point of intersection.

- Instruct students to check the solution on the Home screen and change it to a fraction.

Applying the Concept

Have students work with a partner to solve these equations using intersect and traditional algebra.

    a. $3x + 5 = -2x - 6$ **b.** $1.2x - 6.88 = 9.7x + 15.2$

- Tell students to first simplify the equations by combining like terms so that the x's are on one side of the equation and the constants are on the other.

- Reminds students to create one graph of the coefficient and variable and another graph of the constant.

Step 2

Have student volunteers present both ways on the overhead and projected graphing calculator. Ask the students which method was easier, and why.

Step 3

Have students complete the activity sheet, *Check It Out!* (page 71) for practice in solving linear equations and using the graphing calculator to check the solutions.

Extension Ideas

If students are having difficulty combining like terms to simplify the equations, make it more concrete by using algebra tiles to represent the variables and constants.

- Use the *Algebra Tiles* template (page 215) if you do not have a classroom set of this manipulative. Color one side of the manipulatives blue for positive values and the other side of the manipulatives red for negative values.

- The rectangles represent x and the small squares represent the constants. Use a piece of yarn or paper to represent the equal sign.

Name _____

Date _____

Check It Out!

Directions: Solve each of the equations algebraically, showing all steps. Then, check your answer graphically. For each, record the equations entered into the calculator, the window used to find the solution, the graph, and the point that shows the solution. If you use the Intersect feature on the calculator, be sure to change any decimals into fractions on the Home screen.

a. $11x = -6$

Solution	Graph
Equations	
$Y_1 =$	
$Y_2 =$	
Window Values	
$X[\quad , \quad] \qquad Y[\quad , \quad]$	

b. $7x = 39$

Solution	Graph
Equations	
$Y_1 =$	
$Y_2 =$	
Window Values	
$X[\quad , \quad] \qquad Y[\quad , \quad]$	

Name _____

Date _____

Check It Out! (cont.)

c. $4x + 5 = 9x - 10$

Solution	Graph
Equations $Y_1 =$ $Y_2 =$	
Window Values $X[\quad , \quad]$ $\quad Y[\quad , \quad]$	

d. $-9.2x - 8.56 = 2.3x + 12.5$

Solution	Graph
Equations $Y_1 =$ $Y_2 =$	
Window Values $X[\quad , \quad]$ $\quad Y[\quad , \quad]$	

e. $.29x = 3x - 6.1$

Solution	Graph
Equations $Y_1 =$ $Y_2 =$	
Window Values $X[\quad , \quad]$ $\quad Y[\quad , \quad]$	

Analyzing Constant Change & Straightness

Unit 2

Lesson Description

- Students will fit a line to the plot and understand that the slope of the line equals the vertical change over the horizontal change.
- Students will apply the concept of slope to a real-life scenario.

Materials

- *Up, Down, & Across* (page 79; unt2.79.pdf)
- *Changes* (pages 80–81; unt2.80.pdf)
- TI-83/84 Plus Family Graphing Calculator or TI-73 Explorer™

Using the Calculator

Step 1   Illustrate how to prepare lists.

- To access the Home screen, **QUIT** by pressing **2ND** and then **MODE**. To clear the Home screen, press **CLEAR** twice.

- Ensure that Lists **L1**, **L2**, and **L3** are available by pressing **STAT**, **5** to paste the command. **SetUpEditor** will appear on the Home screen. Press **ENTER** to execute the command.

- Clear **L1–L3** by pressing **STAT**, **4** to paste the **ClrList** command to the Home screen.

- Input **L1**, **L2**, **L3** by pressing **2ND**, **1**, **,**, **2ND**, **2**, **,**, **2ND**, **3**, and then press **ENTER** to execute the command.

Step 2   Model how to enter the data into the Stat List editor.

- Access the Stat List editor in the Stat menu by pressing **STAT** and then **ENTER**.

- Enter the following lists. Move the cursor to the appropriate column, type the numbers, (without commas) and press **ENTER** after each.

> L1 = {1, 2, 3, 4, 5}   L2 = {5, 6, 7, 8, 9}
>
> L3 = {10, 8, 6, 4, 2}

Step 1

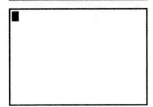

Step 1 *(cont.)*

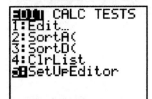

Step 1 *(cont.)*

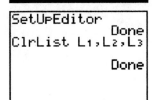

Step 2

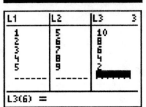

Analyzing Constant Change & Straightness *(cont.)*

Unit 2

Using the Calculator *(cont.)*

Step 3

Show the students how to set up a scatter plot.

- To access the Stat Plot menu, press **2ND** and then **Y=**.

- Press **1** to select **Plot1**. Set it up as shown in the screen shot.

- Highlight each of the following options and press **ENTER** to select it. Select **On**; by **Type:** select the first icon, and by **Mark:** select the first icon.

- Input **L1** for the **Xlist** (**2ND**, **1**), and input **L2** for **Ylist** (**2ND**, **2**).

Step 4

Use the same method to set up Plot 2.

- Input **L1** (**2ND**, **1**) for **Xlist** and **L3** (**2ND**, **2**) for **Ylist**.

- By **Mark**, select the second icon.

Step 5

Show students how to graph in a Standard window.

- Press **ZOOM** and press **6** to select **ZStandard** to set up the following values.

- Press **WINDOW** to see the values shown in the screen shot.

Explaining the Concept

Step 1

Ask the students the following questions. Have them demonstrate the answers using their arms to represent the lines.

- What does it mean for lines to rise and fall? *Answer: A line is falling if the y-values are decreasing left to right. A line is rising if the y-values are increasing from right to left.*

- What does it means for a line to be vertical or horizontal? *Answer: In a vertical line, the x-values are constant and do not change. In a horizontal line, the y-values are constant and do not change.*

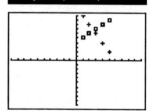

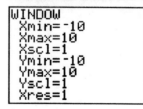

Analyzing Constant Change & Straightness *(cont.)*

Unit 2

Explaining the Concept *(cont.)*

Step 2   Have the students turn off Plot 2 and graph on Plot 1.

- To turn a plot on or off, press **2ND** and then **Y=** to access the Stat Plot menu.

- Press **2**. Highlight **Off**, and press **ENTER** to select it.

- Press **GRAPH** to view **Plot1**.

Step 3   Ask students the following questions related to Plot 1. Test student choices.

- Is it possible to draw a straight line through these points? Why or why not? *Answer: Yes, because the x- and y-values are increasing at a constant rate of change.*

- Is the line rising or falling? Why? *Answer: The line is rising because the y-values are increasing from left to right by 1.*

- Name a pair of x- and y-values that are on the line. *Answers may vary, e.g., (6, 10).* How did you make your choice? *(Test student choices on the projected graphing calculator.)*

- Name a pair of x- and y-values that are not on the line. *Answers may vary, e.g., (3, 2).* How did you make your choice? *(Test student choices on the projected graphing calculator.)*

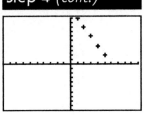

Step 4   Have the students turn off Plot 1 and turn on Plot 2.

- Graph Plot 2 in a Standard window.

Step 5   Ask the students the following questions related to Plot 2. Test students choices on the projected graphing calculator.

- Is it possible to draw a line through these points? Why or why not? *Answer: Yes, because the x- and y-values are decreasing at a constant rate.*

- Name a pair of x and y-values that are on the line. *Answers may vary, e.g., (0, 6).* How did you make your choice? *(Test their answers on the projected graphing calculator.)*

Analyzing Constant Change & Straightness *(cont.)*

Unit 2

Explaining the Concept *(cont.)*

Step 6

Continue to ask students the following questions about Plot 2.

- Name a pair of *x*- and *y*-values that are not on the line. *Answers may vary, e.g., (8, 0)*. How did you make your choice? (Test their choices on the projected graphing calculator.)

- Does this line rise or fall? Why? *Answer: It falls because the slope is decreasing from left to right by two.*

Step 7

Have the students work in pairs to complete the activity sheet *Up, Down, & Across* (page 79).

- Choose students to share their conclusions on the projected graphing calculator.

Applying the Concept

Step 1

Ask the students to tell whether each line is rising, falling, or horizontal.

- The distance vs. time graph of a parked car. *Answer: Horizontal*

- The graph of the charges vs. time for a plumber charging $50 for traveling to the customer's home plus $30 per hour. *Answer: Rising*

- The graph of the student's grade over time if the teacher takes away 1 percentage point from the final grade. *Answer: Falling*

Step 2

Discuss the meaning of *per* in the examples above. Explain that a synonym for *per* is *each*.

Step 3

Have students work in small groups to write their own situations to represent rising and falling lines, or vertical and horizontal lines.

Step 4

Have students complete the activity sheet, *Changes* (pages 80–81).

Extension Ideas

- Have students graph Plot 1 and Plot 2 together using the values given for L1, L2, and L3 in the lesson on page 75. Have them compare and contrast the slope of the lines. Have students calculate the slope for each line.

- Have students differentiate between lines and curves. Explain that an equation of a curve has exponents or a constant that is divided by a variable. Have students use their graphing calculators to graph equations of lines and curves.

Name _____

Date _____

Up, Down, & Across

Directions: Follow the steps below and answer the questions.

a. Clear L1–L6 on your graphing calculator. Enter the following values.

$$L1 = \{10, 6, 2, -2, -6\} \qquad L2 = \{-3, 0, 3, 6, 9\}$$

b. Will the coordinates entered into L1 and L2 form a line? Why or Why not?

_____

_____

c. Create a scatter plot in Plot 1 with L1 for the Xlist and L2 for the Ylist. Be sure all other stat plots are off. Graph the plot in a Standard window.

d. Does this line rise or fall? Explain your answer in terms of the lists.

_____

_____

e. Find an ordered pair that is on the line that would be visible in the Standard window. (You may need to use decimals.) Add the x-coordinate to L1 and the y-coordinate to L2 and regraph to test your point. Explain how you chose your point.

_____

_____

f. Find another ordered pair that is *not* on the line and record it below.

_____

g. Pick a number between –10 and 10. In L3, make a list where every entry is that number. Be sure that you have the same number of entries in L3 and L1. Change Plot 1 so that the Xlist is L1 and the Ylist is L3. Graph the scatter plot. What kind of line goes through these points?

_____

h. Create another scatter plot in Plot 2 where the Xlist is L3 and the Ylist is L1. Graph the scatter plot. What kind of line goes through these points?

_____

i. How can you tell from the lists that a line will rise from left to right? Fall from left to right? Be horizontal? Be vertical?

_____

_____

Name _____

Date _____

Changes

Directions: Follow the steps below to set up the graphing calculator.

a. Enter the following values in **L1 = {0, 1, 2, 3, 4, 5, 6, 7, 8, 9, 10}**.

b. You are on the sidewalk in front of your home, walking forward at 400 ft/min. In L2, enter the distance that you would have traveled after 0, 1, 2, 3, 4 minutes, etc.

c. Create a scatter plot in Plot 1 of the data in L1 and L2, and input the window values shown below on the graphing calculator.

Xmin = –10 Xmax = 10 Xscl = 1 Ymin = –4000

Ymax = 4000 Yscl = 400 Xres = 1

d. Graph the scatter plot and sketch your graph below. Label the axes *time* (*x*) and *distance* (*y*) and indicate the scale on each axis.

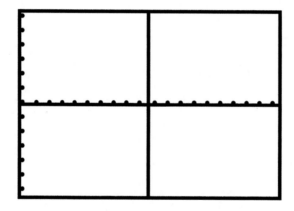

e. On the number line below, mark your position after one minute with an *a*, after 2 minutes with a *b*, after 3 minutes with a *c*, and so on for all 10 minutes.

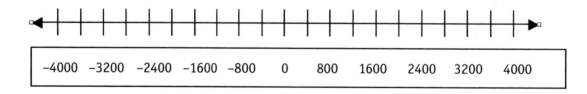

| –4000 | –3200 | –2400 | –1600 | –800 | 0 | 800 | 1600 | 2400 | 3200 | 4000 |

f. Suppose, instead of walking forward, you walked backward. Although the distance traveled would be the same, your position would be in the opposite direction. Mark your positions on the number line using *a*, *b*, *c*, etc. to mark your positions on the left side of 0.

Changes *(cont.)*

g. In L3, enter the position from walking backward for each time in L1. (These will be negative numbers.)

h. Make a scatter plot in Plot 2 with L1 for the Xlist and L3 for the YList. Leave Plot 1 turned on. Sketch your graph below, labeling the axes *time* (*x*) and *distance* (*y*) and indicating the scale on each axis.

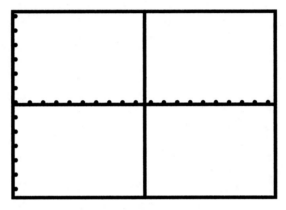

i. How are Plot 1 and Plot 2 different? How are they the same?

_____

_____

j. Are the lines in Plot 1 and Plot 2 rising or falling? Why?

_____

_____

Directions: This activity illustrates the difference between speed and velocity. Answer the questions to discover the difference for yourself.

k. Speed is distance traveled per unit of time. The values for speed are always positive, no matter in what direction the object is traveling. What is the speed for walking forward and backward?

_____

_____

l. Velocity indicates the direction of travel. If the velocity for walking forward is 400 ft/min, what is the velocity for walking backward?

_____

Exploring Slope as a Constant Rate of Change

Unit 2

Lesson Description

- Students will solve real-life scenario problems involving rates, average speed, distance, and time.
- Students will note that on graphs of linear functions, the vertical change (change in *y*-value) per unit of horizontal change (change in *x*-value) is always the same, and that the ratio ("rise over run") is the slope of a graph.

Materials

- Stop-watches
- Long centimeter measuring tapes
- Roll of bulletin board paper or butcher paper
- *Baby Steps* (pages 86–87; unt2.86.pdf)
- *Walk This Way!* (page 88; unt2.88.pdf)
- **Appendix C:** Using the CBR2 with Easy Data (page 216; appnd216.pdf)
- **Appendix C:** CBL/CBR with Temperature Probe and CBR Sensor (pages 217–219; appnd217.pdf)
- TI-83/84 Plus Family Graphing Calculator or TI-73 Explorer™

Step 1

Explaining the Concept/Using the Calculator

As a class, follow the steps below to collect time versus distance data. Pass out the activity sheet, *Baby Steps* (pages 86–87).

- Have a student walk forward and backward along the paper. As the student walks, have another student call out the elapsed time in seconds.
- Other students should be positioned along the paper to mark the walker's position at each second. The starting position should be marked as *t* = 0, the first second *t* = 1, etc.
- Instruct the student to walk slowly away from the end of the paper for a few seconds, stand still for a few seconds, and then walk closer to the end of the paper for a few seconds. The walker should try to maintain a steady pace for each part.
- Measure the distance from the end of the paper to each mark made by the students.
- Repeat the process a few times, or if there is enough space, have several groups collect data.

Exploring Slope as a Constant Rate of Change *(cont.)*

Unit 2

Explaining the Concept/Using the Calculator *(cont.)*

Step 2

Have students enter the data into the graphing calculator using different calculators for different data sets.

- Press **STAT**, **5** and then **ENTER** to access the **SetUpEditor**, and setup lists **L1–L6**.

- Press **STAT**, **1** to access the Stat List editor.

- Clear lists **L1–L6** by using the up arrow to highlight the list name and pressing **CLEAR** and then **ENTER**.

- In **L1**, enter the following times in seconds, by typing each number and then pressing **ENTER**. Then, enter the distances into **L2**.

$$\{0, 1, 2, 3, 4, 5, \text{etc.}\}$$

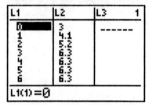

Step 3

Have students set up the graphing calculator to create a Stat Plot.

- Press **MODE** and be sure that the default settings are chosen so that all the selections to the left are highlighted.

- Access the **FORMAT** by pressing **2ND** and then **ZOOM**. Ensure that all default settings (all left side settings) are selected.

Step 4

Model how to create a line graph of the data.

- Press **Y=** and **CLEAR** to clear any equations entered.

- Press **2ND** and then **Y=** to access the Stat Plot editor.

- Press **1** to select **Plot1**.

- Select the following options by highlighting them and pressing **ENTER**. Turn **On** Plot1. By **Type:** select the second icon.

- By **Mark:** select the first icons.

- By **Xlist:** enter **L1** (**2ND**, **1**). By **Ylist:** enter **L2** (**2ND**, **2**).

Exploring Slope as a Constant Rate of Change *(cont.)*
Unit 2

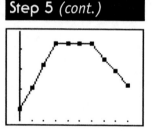

Explaining the Concept/Using the Calculator *(cont.)*

Step 5 Set up an appropriate window and create the graph.

- Press ▨ and then 「9」 to create a ZoomStat window.

- The graph will appear on the screen.

Step 6 Ask the following questions about the graph.

- What does the *x*-axis represent? The *y*-axis?

- What are the units of measure on each axis?

- Was the student moving at a steady rate? How can you tell?

- When was the distance between the student and the end of the paper increasing? Decreasing? How can you tell? (It is important to describe the distance as increasing or decreasing instead of forward or backward motion.)

Step 5 *(cont.)*

- How fast was the student moving on the three parts of the graph? Be sure to use correct units of measure. Be sure to select the points used to compute the velocity from right to left, so that the velocity of the last section is negative.

- Ask the students how you can tell where velocity is negative just by looking at the graph. What was happening to the distance at that time?

- Repeat the above questions with the other graphs after linking them to the teacher's graphing calculator or by using Presentation Link with TI-84 calculators.

Step 7 Have students complete the activity sheet, *Walk This Way!* (page 88).

Applying the Concept

Step 1 Share with students the following problem.

The speed skater, Rebekah Bradford, finished a 500 meter race in 42 seconds flat. She completed the first lap in 8.75 seconds, the second lap in 7.75 seconds, the third lap in 8.5 seconds, the fourth lap in 8.25 seconds, and the fifth lap in 8.75 seconds.

Exploring Slope as a Constant Rate of Change *(cont.)*

Unit 2

Step 2

Applying the Concept *(cont.)*

Together, create a scatter plot of the data.

- In **L1** enter the number of total seconds that have elapsed at the end of each lap, beginning with 0 for the start of the race.
- In **L2** enter 0, 100, 200, 300, 400, and 500, the total distance of the run.
- Press ▣ᶻᵒᵒᴹ and select **9: ZoomStat** to create a ZoomStat window.

Step 3

Ask students the following questions about the data.

- How would you describe Rebekah's pace throughout the race? *Answer: Her second lap was the fastest, followed by the fourth, and then the third and the first.*
- How does the graph show the changes in velocity? *Answer: She is going the fastest where the lines are the steepest.*
- What is Rebekah's velocity for each lap? *Answer: Lap 1: .0875 m/s, lap 2: .0775 m/sec, lap 3: .08 m/sec, lap 4: .0825 m/sec*
- How would Rebekah possibly use this data to prepare for her next race? *Answers may vary. A possible answer is that she may decide that she needs to get off to a better start.*

Step 4

Have students in small groups brainstorm a sport that would benefit from analyzing velocity and speed data.

- Have students choose and write a scenario describing the motion of the athlete playing that sport.
- Have students create velocity and speed graphs to represent the athlete's motion.
- Have small groups trade scenarios, but not graphs. Have each group create a graph for the scenario they received.
- Have small groups compare the graphs for each scenario.

Extension Ideas

- Have the students think of real-life scenarios to represent the graphs on *Walk This Way!* (page 88).
- Have each group repeat the activity using the CBR (Calculator Based Ranger). The CBR is a motion detector that connects to the calculator and measures the student's distance from the CBR and creates a time-distance graph. If you have one CBR, have one group complete the activity for the class, using a projected graphing calculator.

Name _____

Date _____

Baby Steps

Directions: Working in a small group or with the whole class, follow the steps below to collect time versus distance data.

Materials
- Stop watches
- Long centimeter measuring tapes
- Roll of bulletin board paper or butcher paper

Procedure

1. One student should walk forward and backward along the paper.

2. As the student walks, another student should call out the elapsed time in seconds.

3. Other students should position themselves along the paper to mark the walker's position at each second. The starting position should be marked as $t = 0$, the first second $t = 1$, and so on.

4. The person walking should walk slowly away from the end of the paper for a few seconds, stand still for a few seconds, and then walk closer to the end of the paper for a few seconds. The walker should try to maintain a steady pace for each part.

5. Measure the distance from the end of the paper to each mark made by the students.

6. On the graphing calculator, enter the time in L1 and the distance in L2 of the Stat List editor. Create a scatter plot of the data in an appropriate window.

7. Draw the scatter plot in the box below.

Name _____

Date _____

Baby Steps *(cont.)*

Directions: Answer the questions about the scatter plot.

a. What do the *x*- and *y*-axes represent? What are the units of measure on each axis?

_____

_____

_____

b. Was the student moving at a steady rate? How can you tell?

_____

_____

_____

c. When is the distance between the student and the end of the paper increasing? When is it decreasing? How can you tell?

_____

_____

_____

d. How fast was the student moving on the three parts of the graph?

_____

_____

_____

e. Just by looking at the graph, how you can tell where velocity is negative? What was happening to the distance at that time?

Hint: Be sure to select the points used to compute the velocity from right to left so that the velocity of the last section is negative.

_____

_____

_____

Name _____

Date _____

Walk This Way!

Directions: The graphs below were created by a student walking and graphing his time vs. his distance. For each graph, describe the walker's motion, give the time and position when the student stopped or changed direction, and find the velocity for each of the three segments of the graph. Be sure to tell when the distance is increasing and when it is decreasing.

a.

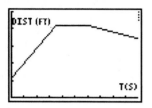

_____

_____

_____

_____

b.

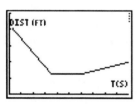

_____

_____

_____

_____

c.

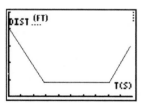

_____

_____

_____

_____

d.

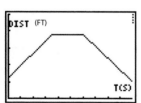

_____

_____

_____

_____

Constructing Slope-Intercept Form

Unit 2

Lesson Description

- Students will write linear equations and express them in slope-intercept form.
- Students will use slope and *y*-intercept to graph linear equations.

Materials

- *Linear Equations* (page 96; unt2.96.pdf)
- *Graph It* (page 97; unt2.97.pdf)
- TI-83/84 Plus Family Graphing Calculator or TI-73 Explorer™

Step 1

Explaining the Concept

Review linear equations with the students.

- Write the following equations on the board.

$$3x - y = 4 \qquad y = 3x - 4 \qquad \frac{3x}{4} - \frac{y}{4} = 1$$

- Ask students, "Which of these equations has a graph that is a line?" *Answer: All three.*

- Most students will recognize that the first two are lines, but may be uncertain about the third.

- Emphasize that for an equation to have a graph of a line, the variables can have no exponents other than one, and the variables cannot be in the denominator of a fraction.

Step 2

Ask the class which one of the equations above they believe would be the easiest to graph.

- Explain that most people choose the second one because *y* is expressed in terms of *x*. This makes it easy to make a table of ordered pairs.

Step 3

Read step **a** on the activity sheet, *Linear Equations* (page 96). Have students plug the *x*-values into the equation $y = 3x - 4$.

- Make certain the students understand that the constant change in the *y*-values is significant only because the *x*-values are increasing by the same amount each time.

Constructing Slope-Intercept Form *(cont.)*

Unit 2

Step 4

Step 1

Step 2

Explaining the Concept *(cont.)*

Have students complete step *b* on the activity sheet, *Linear Equations* (page 96).

- Discuss students' responses. Students should state that there is a constant change in the *y*-values or that the *y*-values are increasing by three.

- Read step **c** on the activity sheet and fill in the next two columns on the table.

- Answer the question for step **d** on the activity sheet, *Linear Equations*.

- Emphasize the fact that the same *x* and *y* make all three equations true, meaning that they are equivalent equations; that is to say, there are three different forms of the same equation.

- Tell the students that each form is useful for a different purpose.

Using the Calculator

Create a scatter plot using the data in the table on the activity sheet, *Linear Equations*.

- Press **2ND** and then **Y=** to access the Stat Plot menu. Choose **1: Plot1**.

- Select the following settings by highlighting each and pressing **ENTER**. Turn **On** Plot1. By **Type:** select the first icon.

- Input **L1** (**2ND**, **1**) for **Xlist**. Input **L2** (**2ND**, **2**) for **Ylist**.

- By **Mark:** select the first icon.

Model how to set up lists in the Stat List editor.

- Use **SetUpEditor** to ensure that lists **L1–L6** are available by pressing **STAT**, **5**, and then **ENTER**.

- Access the Stat List editor by pressing **STAT** and then **ENTER**.

- Clear lists **L1–L4** by moving the cursor over the name, press **CLEAR**, and then **ENTER**.

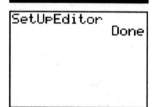

Constructing Slope-Intercept Form *(cont.)*

Unit 2

Using the Calculator *(cont.)*

Step 3 | Enter the values given in the first column of the table on *Linear Equations* (page 96) into L1 of the Stat List editor.

- Position the cursor below **L1**, type the value and press **ENTER** after each, e.g., (-), 2, **ENTER**, (-), 1, **ENTER**.

Step 4 | Model how to enter a list formula into the Stat List editor.

- Input the formula **3L1–4** into **L2** by moving the cursor onto **L2**, and press **ENTER**. (**L1** is accessed by pressing **2ND** followed by 1.)
- Graph the scatter plot by choosing **ZOOM** and then **6: ZStandard**.

Step 5 | Model how to create a graph for the line $y = 3x - 4$ over the scatter plot.

- Press **Y=** and clear any equations entered.
- Input **3x – 4** next to **Y₁**. **Plot1** should be highlighted at the top to indicate that it is turned on.
- Press **GRAPH** to view the line superimposed on the scatter plot.

Special Note: The scatter plot allows the students to trace the exact points without adjusting the window and will be used to investigate slope in Step 9.

Step 6 | Analyze the scatter plot and graph of the line.

- Press **TRACE**. Use the right left arrows to investigate the points.
- Use the down arrows to switch between the scatter plot and the line. The upper left corner of the screen shows the equation being traced.
- Explain that tracing the scatter plot displays the values entered in the lists, but tracing on the line displays points chosen according to *x*-values predetermined by the size of the screen.

Steps 3 & 4

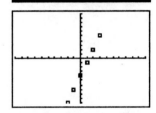

Step 4 *(cont.)*

Step 4 *(cont.)*

Step 5

Steps 5 & 6 *(cont.)*

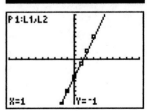

Lesson 8

Constructing Slope-Intercept
Form *(cont.)*
Unit 2

Using the Calculator *(cont.)*

Step 7

Model how to identify the *y*-intercept on both the scatter plot and the line.

- Ask students to trace to the point where the line crosses the *y*-axis and record it for question **e** on *Linear Equations* activity sheet (page 96). *Answer: (0, –4)*

- Explain that this particular point should be the same on either the scatter plot or the line, but this is not always the case.

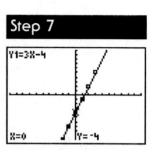

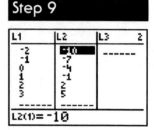

Step 8

Have students graph other lines and consider the ordered pairs of the *y*-intercepts.

- Explain that the *y*-intercept is always identified by its *y*-coordinate because the *x*-coordinate is always zero.

Step 9

Model how to determine the slope of $y = 3x - 4$.

- Return to the Stat List editor by pressing [STAT] and then [ENTER].

- Ask the class to identify which list shown on the scatter plot contains the *x*- and *y*-values. *Answer: x-values = L1 and y-values = L2*

Step 10

Model how to choose two pairs of points and calculate the slope between them.

- To find the slope, divide the change in *y* by the change in *x*.

$$m = \frac{y_2 - y_1}{x_2 - x_1}.$$

- Because this change in a variable is so important, mathematicians use the delta symbol, Δ, to represent it. Rewrite the slope formula as $m = \frac{\Delta y}{\Delta x}$.

Step 11

Explain that the calculator has a built-in way of subtracting consecutive numbers in a list. This is called ΔList.

- Have students work with a partner to rewrite $\frac{\Delta y}{\Delta x}$ as a list formula.

$$\frac{\Delta \text{List}(L2)}{\Delta \text{List}(L1)}$$

Constructing Slope-Intercept Form *(cont.)*

Unit 2

Using the Calculator *(cont.)*

Step 12   Have students enter the formula "ΔList(L2)/ΔList (L1)" into **L3**.

- Press **ALPHA** and then **+** to access the quotes. The quotes allow the list to update **L3** if **L1** and/or **L2** are changed.

- Press **2ND** followed by **STAT**, highlight **OPS** and press **7** to select Δ**List**.

- Press **2ND**, **2**, **)** for (**L2**). Press **÷**.

- Insert Δ**List** again. Press **2ND**, **1**, **)** for (**L1**).

- Press **ENTER** to execute the command. Notice that the slope for each pair of points is displayed. L3 has one less entry than L1 and L2 because of the pairing of the numbers.

- Have the students enter the slope for question **e** on the activity sheet, *Linear Equations* (page 96).

Step 13   Lead students to discover the slope-intercept form using the equation $y = -2x + 3$.

- Enter the formula **−2L1+3** (no quotes) into **L2** by pressing **(-)** **2**, **2ND**, **1**, **+**, **3**.

- **IMPORTANT:** Do **NOT** clear **L2** first. It will cause a problem with the values in L3. If you do, you must clear L3 and start over.

- Write the slope of the line for question **e** on the activity sheet, *Linear Equations* (page 96).

- Enter the corresponding equation in **Y₁** and graph it in a ZStandard window (**ZOOM**, **6**).

- Find the *y*-intercept and write it on the table below step **f** on the *Linear Equations* activity sheet.

Step 12

L1	L2	L3	▸3
-2	-10	3	
-1	-7	3	
0	-4	3	
1	-1	3	
3	2		
	5		

L3 ="ΔList(L2)/ΔL

Step 12 *(cont.)*

NAMES **OPS** MATH
1:SortA(
2:SortD(
3:dim(
4:Fill(
5:seq(
6:cumSum(
7▮ΔList(

Step 12 *(cont.)*

L1	L2	L3	▸3
-2	-10	3	
-1	-7	3	
0	-4	3	
1	-1	3	
2	2		
3	5		

L3(1)=3

Step 13

L1	L2	L3	▸2
-2	7	-2	
-1	5	-2	
0	3	-2	
1	1	-2	
2	-1	-2	
3	-3		

L2(1)=7

Step 13 *(cont.)*

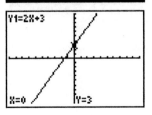

Constructing Slope-Intercept Form *(cont.)*

Unit 2

Using the Calculator *(cont.)*

Step 14

Have students complete the table below step **g** on the *Linear Equations* activity sheet (page 96).

- Have students write three more equations, change the formula in L2, and determine the slopes and the *y*-intercepts.

- When students are finished with this task, they should clear L3 on their calculators. Failure to do so will cause error messages in the future.

Step 15

Tell the students that they have been looking at equations of lines expressed in slope-intercept form, $y = mx + b$.

- Explain that *m* is generally used for slope and *b* for the *y*-intercept.

- Have students complete the table below step **g** on the *Linear Equations* activity sheet.

- Discuss the equation $y = 5$. Point out that it could be written $y = 0x + 5$.

- Write $y = \frac{2}{3} x - 3$ on the board. Ask what the slope of $\frac{2}{3}$ means.

Applying the Concept

Step 1

Have students graph $y = 3x - 4$ by hand.

- Have the students draw a set of axes, approximately −10 to 10 in each direction, and put a dot on the *y*-axis to represent the *y*-intercept.

- Explain that the slope of 3 could be written as $\frac{3}{1}$, and they should interpret this as the change in *y* over the change in *x*.

- Instruct the students to put the pencil point on the *y*-intercept and move up three spaces and then to the right one space and draw a point. Have them repeat the process and draw a line.

- Caution the students not to count 1 until they have moved a space.

#50024—Graphing Calculator Strategies, Algebra   © *Shell Education*

Constructing Slope-Intercept Form *(cont.)*

Unit 2

Step 2

Applying the Concept *(cont.)*

Students should graph the equations in table **g** on the *Linear Equations* activity sheet.

- Show the students that a slope of –3 can be interpreted as either

$$\frac{-3}{1} \text{ or } \frac{3}{-1}$$

- Have students graph both equations to see if they are the same line.
- Ask the students how to write 0 as a fraction. Explain that *y* never changes and that they are just moving in a horizontal direction.
- Discuss why vertical lines cannot be expressed in slope-intercept form.
- Point out that the fraction $\frac{2}{3}$ could also be written as $\frac{-2}{-3}$.

Step 3

Have students complete the activity sheet, *Graph It* (page 97).

- Have students work in small groups to present their answers on the chart.
- Then have students decorate the chart paper with artistic elements that represent linear equations, slope, and *y*-intercept.

Extension Ideas

- Have students answer the question, "Why do you think slope-intercept form of the equation of a line is used most frequently?"
- Have students determine how slope–intercept form would apply to problems dealing with rates; e.g., a plumber charges $25 per hour plus an additional fee of $30 for driving to your home.
- Have students research other forms for expressing the equations of lines.

Name _____

Date _____

Linear Equations

Directions: Follow the steps below.

a. Complete the second column of the table by inputting the values for x into the equation $y = 3x - 4$.

x	y	$3x - y$	$\dfrac{3x}{4} - \dfrac{y}{4}$
−2			
−1			
0			
1			
2			
3			

b. How do the y-values demonstrate that the equation $y = 3x - 4$ is a line?

c. Complete the last two columns by inputting the values for x and y into the equations.

d. What do the values in the table tell you about the equations below?

$$3x - y = 4 \qquad y = 3x - 4 \qquad \frac{3x}{4} - \frac{y}{4} = 1$$

_____

e. What is the slope and y-intercept of $y = 3x - 4$ and $y = -2x + 3$?

_____

f. Graph three equations and identify the slope and y-intercept of each.

Equation	Slope	y-intercept

g. Complete the chart and graph each line on the graphing calculator.

Equation	Slope	y-intercept
$y = 4x - 5$		
$y = -3x + 8$		
$y = 5$		
$y = \dfrac{2}{3}x - 3$		

Name

Date

Graph It

Directions: For each equation, give the *y*-intercept and the slope, and sketch the graph. Check the *y*-intercept and slope by graphing the equation on your calculator, using a ZStandard window.

a. $y = 5x - 2$

slope _____ *y*-intercept _____

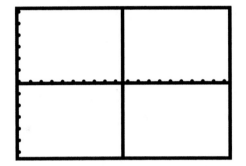

b. $y = \frac{-1}{5}x - 2$

slope _____ *y*-intercept _____

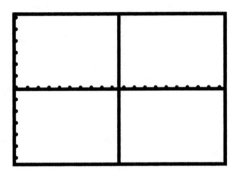

c. $y = -2x + 6$

slope _____ *y*-intercept _____

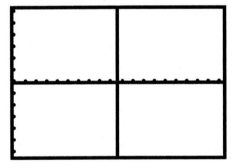

d. $y = 4x - 6$

slope _____ *y*-intercept _____

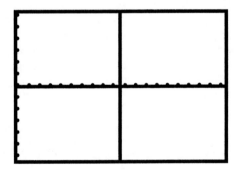

e. $y = 8$

slope _____ *y*-intercept _____

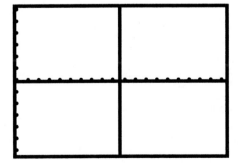

f. $y = 0$

slope _____ *y*-intercept _____

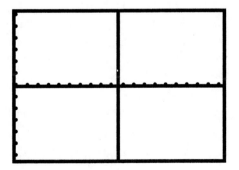

Solving One-Variable Inequalities

Unit 2

Step 1

Lesson Description

- Students will learn to graph and solve one-variable inequalities.
- Students will solve multistep problems, involving linear inequalities with one variable.

Materials

- *Graphing Inequalities* (pages 104–105; unt2.104.pdf)
- *At The Movies* (page 106; unt2.106.pdf)
- TI-83/84 Plus Family Graphing Calculator or TI-73 Explorer™

Explaining the Concept

Explain how to graph inequalities on a number line using the inequalities below.

a. $x > -4$

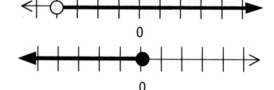

0

b. $a \leq 0$

0

- Explain that an open circle represents less than (<) or greater than (>). These symbols indicate that the end point is not included in the graph. This is called a strict inequality.

- Explain that a closed circle represents less than or equal to (≤) and greater than or equal to (≥). These symbols indicate that the end point is included in the graph. This is called a conditional inequality.

- Point out that number lines can be either vertical, such as a thermometer, or horizontal. Instruct two volunteers to illustrate both of these on the board or overhead.

Step 2

Discuss the height limits on rides at amusement parks.

- Describe signs that say that the rider must be at least, more than, at most, and less than 56 inches tall to ride. Discuss what these mean in terms of inequalities.

- Have students complete the inequalities and the number lines for problems **a–d** on the activity sheet, *Graphing Inequalities* (page 104).

- Explain that any number in the shaded region is a solution to the inequality.

Solving One-Variable Inequalities *(cont.)*

Unit 2

Explaining the Concept *(cont.)*

Step 3

Introduce how to solve linear inequalities by modeling the problem below.

c. $-2x + 5 < -1$

$\ \ -5\ \ -5$

$\dfrac{-2x < -6}{-2 \quad\ -2}$

$\ \ x > 3$

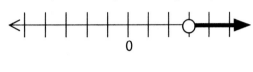

- Show the students that solving a linear inequality involving addition and subtraction is just like solving a linear equation, and whatever is done on one side of the inequality, should be done to the other.

- Model how to shade the arrows on the number line to indicate that the solutions represent infinity.

- Tell students that sometimes they may have to multiply or divide to isolate a variable. In both inequalities and equations, they should multiply and divide both sides by the same number. Remind students that when dividing by a negative, the inequality sign switches.

Step 4

Have the students solve the linear equations and graph the solutions for problems **e–h** on the activity sheet, *Graphing Inequalities* (page 105).

Using the Calculator

Step 1

Have students solve the following inequality.

d. $x + 4 < 10$

$\ \ -4\ \ -4$

$\ \ x < 6$

- Have students pick two numbers that are solutions and two numbers that are not solutions.

Step 2

Model how to store a value for *x*.

- Input a chosen solution, e.g., **2**. Press (**2**), **STO›** .

- Press **X,T,Ø,n** and then **ENTER** to store the value for *x*.

Step 2
2→X
■ 2

Solving One-variable Inequalities *(cont.)*

Unit 2

Using the Calculator *(cont.)*

Step 3

Substitute the solution for *x* in the inequality, $x + 4 < 10$ and check the solution using Boolean Logic.

- On the Home screen, input **x + 4** by pressing **X,T,θ,n**, **+**, and **4**.
- Press **2ND** and **MATH** to access **TEST**.
- Press **5** to paste **<** to the Home screen and then type **10**.
- Press **ENTER** to execute the command. The inequality signs will produce an answer of **1** if the solution is true, or **0** if the solution is false.

Step 4

Have students check the solutions to the linear equalities they solved on the activity sheet, *Graphing Inequalities* (page 104) in a similar fashion.

Step 5

Model how to use the Test menu to graph simple inequalities.

- Press **Y=**. Clear any equations that have been previously entered.
- By **Y₁** input **x < 3**. Access **<** from the **TEST** menu.
- Check that the plots at the top of the screen are turned off (unhighlighted).
- Check **MODE** and **FORMAT** (**2ND**, **ZOOM**) to ensure default settings (left-sides) are selected.

Step 6

View the graph and determine whether the values are solutions.

- Press **ZOOM** and then **4** to select **ZDecimal**. The calculator will create the graph of the inequality in a Decimal window.
- Press **TRACE** to view the values. Point out that the *y*-values are all **0** or **1**, indicating the statement is either false or true.

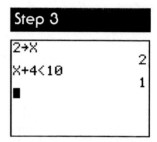

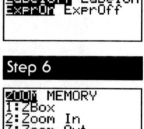

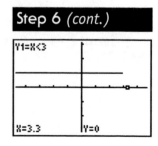

Solving One-Variable Inequalities *(cont.)*

Unit 2

Using the Calculator *(cont.)*

Step 7

Show that the calculator is graphing both parts, true and false, by turning the axes off on the projected graphing calculator.

- To turn the axes off, choose **FORMAT** by pressing **2ND** and then **ZOOM**.
- Highlight **AxesOff**, press **ENTER**, and then **GRAPH**.
- Explain to the students that the false portion was hidden by the *x*-axis.
- Emphasize that this graph shows the *x*-values of the solution to the one-variable inequality.

  Special Note: *Have students turn the axes back on for the next part of the lesson.*

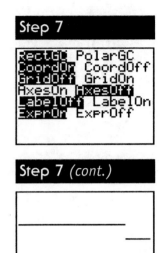

Explaining the Concept/Using the Calculator

Step 1

Ask the students to use their graphing calculators to graph $2x \geq 5$.

- Refer to **Steps 5** and **6** in the **Using the Calculator** section for how to input and graph this equation.
- Have them trace the values to find the solution and then express the inequality as $x \geq 2.5$.
- Ask the students if this was the answer they expected to get.

Step 2

Model how to solve linear inequalities with negative coefficients.

- Ask the students to use their calculators to graph and solve $2x \geq -5$.
- Ask the students if $x \geq -2.5$ was the solution they expected.

Step 3

Ask students to solve $-2x \geq 5$, using their calculators.

- Have the students discuss why the solution, $x \leq -2.5$, has the inequality sign reversed.

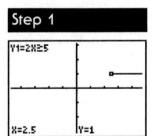

Solving One-Variable Inequalities *(cont.)*

Unit 2

Explaining the Concept/Using the Calculator *(cont.)*

Step 4

Illustrate for students the sign reversal, using two inequalities students know to be true, 8 > 4 and −4 > −8.

- Instruct students to place the numbers 8 and 4 and −8 and −4 on the number line, for problem **i** on the activity sheet *Graphing Inequalities* (page 105). Point out how the left/right relationships indicate the direction of the inequality.

- For problem **j**, have the students divide each number by 2. Students should place the values on the number line and write the inequalities 4 > 2 and −2 > −4.

- Ask students if the quotients maintain the same left/right relationships. Have students record their responses for problem **k**. *Answer: Their relative left/right positions are maintained.*

Step 5

Have the students divide each number by −2.

- Have students place the values on the second number line and write the inequalities −4 < −2 and 2 < 4, for problem **l** on the activity sheet *Graphing Inequalities*.

- Ask students if the quotients maintain the same left/right relationships. Have students record their responses for problem **m**. *Answer: Their relative left/right positions are not maintained because the signs need to be reversed to make these statements true.*

Step 6

Ask the students to predict what will happen if they multiply both sides of an inequality by a negative number.

- Have them test their theory by graphing

  $\frac{-1}{2} x \geq -1$ on their calculators and then solving

  it by multiplying both sides by −2.

- Refer to **Steps 5** and **6** in the **Using the Calculator** section for how to input and graph the equation.

- Ask students to summarize the rule they just tested. *Possible Answer: If you multiply both sides of an inequality by a negative number, you should flip the sign because the direction of the inequality reverses.*

Step 6

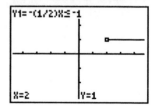

Step 6 *(cont.)*

Solving One-Variable Inequalities *(cont.)*

Unit 2

Applying the Concept

Step 1   Ask the students to formulate the rules for solving linear inequalities and then answer problem **n** on *Graphing Inequalities* (page 105). Be sure that they explain how it is different from solving a linear equation.

Step 2   Ask the students to write and solve an inequality for the following statement.
Jennifer has at least 8 more than twice as many CDs as her brother who has 52 CDs.

- Ask students to identify key words that would help them represent this statement with an inequality.

- Have them explain which symbols would be used to represent them.

Key Word	Symbol
8 more	+ 8
Twice as many	2x
At least	> 52

- Emphasize that there are endless possibilities for the number of Jennifer's CDs.

Step 3   Have students work with a partner or small group to write similar statements. Groups should exchange statements and write inequalities and create graphs to represent the statement they received.

Step 4   Have the students complete the activity sheet, *At The Movies* (page 106) to practice writing, graphing, and solving inequalities.

 ## Extension Idea

- Have students investigate the difference between discrete and continuous solutions by contrasting discrete situations (like the number of tickets sold) and continuous situations (like an amount of time or a pure numerical situation).

Graphing Inequalities

Directions: The following number lines and expressions represent the required height for rides at an amusement park. Write an inequality for the height h on the lines below and then graph each on a vertical and horizontal number line.

a. At least 56 inches

_____

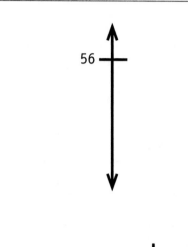

b. More than 56 inches

_____

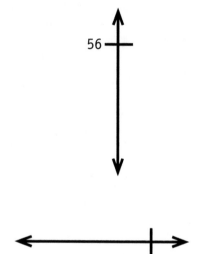

c. At most 56 inches

_____

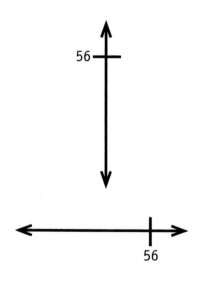

d. Less than 56 inches

_____

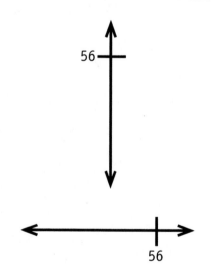

Name _____

Date _____

Graphing Inequalities *(cont.)*

Directions: Solve the inequalities. Graph the solution on the horizontal number line.

e. $x + 7 < 10$

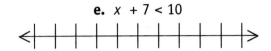

f. $x + 7 \le -10$

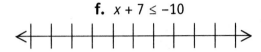

g. $x - 7 > -3$

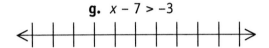

h. $x - 2 \ge 2$

i. Graph the numbers 8, 4, –8, and –4 on the number line below. Write an inequality using 8 and 4 and another using –8 and –4 on the lines next to the number line.

_____

_____

j. Divide each number in the inequalities above by 2. Graph the resulting inequalities on the number line and record the inequalities on the lines next to the number line.

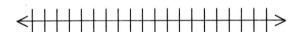

_____

_____

k. Are the directions for the new inequalities in problem **j** the same as those in problem **i**?

_____

l. Divide each number in the original inequalities above by –2. Graph the resulting numbers on the number line and record the inequalities on the lines next to the number line.

_____

_____

m. Are the directions for the new inequalities in problem **l** the same as those in problem **i**?

_____

n. How do you solve a linear inequality? How is it different from solving a linear equation? Explain your answer on a separate piece of paper.

Name _____

Date _____

At the Movies

Directions: Write and graph an inequality to represent each statement. It may be necessary to solve the inequality before you graph it.

a. The matinee at the movie costs $4.50 to get in. You will need popcorn ($2.50) and a soft drink ($1.75) to get through the movie. Write and graph an inequality that describes the cash needed if you wish to attend the movie.

_____

b. All of the movies at the theater begin at 2:30 p.m. It will take 35 minutes to walk home from the theater. Your mother needs you to be home by 5:05 p.m. Write and graph an inequality that describes the length of the movie you can see.

_____

c. If you took a bus, you could get home in less time than the 35 minutes it would take to walk. The exact amount of time will vary, but you know that walking would take you at least 10 minutes more than twice as long as the ride on the bus. Write, solve, and graph an inequality that that describes the length of the bus ride.

_____

d. The day you go to the movies it is very cold. In fact, the temperature is predicted to be –8°, which is no more than 2 degrees less than –.5 times the previous day's temperature. Write, solve, and graph an inequality that describes the previous day's temperature.

_____

Conceptualizing Absolute Value

Unit 2

Lesson 10

Lesson Description

- Students will understand the meaning of the absolute value of a number and interpret the absolute value as the distance of the number from zero on a number line.
- Students will solve equations and inequalities involving absolute values.

Materials

- *Absolute Value* (pages 112–113; unt2.112.pdf)
- *Which Way Did They Go?* (page 114; unt2.114.pdf)
- TI-83/84 Plus Family Graphing Calculator and TI-73 Explorer™

Explaining the Concept

Step 1

Give students a copy of the activity sheet, *Absolute Value* (page 112). Use the activity sheet to introduce the concept of absolute value as distance.

- Think of two places that are approximately the same distance from your school, with one to the east and the other to the west of the school.
- On the number line at the top of the *Absolute Value* activity sheet (page 112), have the students plot the distances using an appropriate scale.
- Explain that we use absolute value to indicate distance on the number line. Point out that just as the directions are opposite, the coordinates on the number line are opposites as well.

Step 2

Illustrate the use of the absolute value symbol.

- Have students complete statements **a–b** on the *Absolute Value* activity sheet.
- Point out that because the absolute value of zero is zero, it is correct to say that the absolute value of *nonnegative numbers* are the same as the correlating negative numbers.

Step 3

Write the expression $|x|$ on the board.

- Ask the students what they would need to know about x to determine whether $|x| = x$ or $|x| = -x$.
- Point out that for nonnegative numbers, values are the same as x, and for negative numbers they are the opposite of x.
- Emphasize that "$-x$" means the opposite of x and may or may not represent a negative number, depending on the value of x.

© Shell Education

#50024—Graphing Calculator Strategies, Algebra

Conceptualizing Absolute Value *(cont.)*

Unit 2

Using the Calculator

Step 1
Show the students how to access the absolute value command on the graphing calculator. There are two ways.

- The first method is to select **MATH**, arrow to **NUM**, and press ⬚**1** to select **abs(**.

- The second method is to select **CATALOG** by pressing **2ND** followed by ⬚**0**. Then press **ENTER**.

- Both methods paste the command **abs(** on the Home screen. To complete the action, input a number following the argument, **abs(**, e.g.,–3. Close the parentheses and press **ENTER**.

- Remind students to press ⬚**(-)** and not **–**.

Step 2
Explain to students that an equation can be used to represent the absolute value of an unknown value. Transfer students' understanding from the concrete to the abstract by having them input values into the equation on the graphing calculator.

Step 3
Ask students how they would write and input an equation to represent the absolute value of *x* on the graphing calculator. *Answer: y = 1 x 1; y = abs (x).*

- Press **Y=**. Delete any previously entered equations by highlighting each and pressing **CLEAR**.

- Enter **abs(x)** into **Y₁**. Press **x,T,θ,n** to access the **x**. Press **)** to close the parentheses.

- Choose **TBLSET** by pressing **2ND** followed by **WINDOW** and enter the settings shown in the screen shot.

- Access **TBL** by pressing **2ND** and then **GRAPH**.

Step 4
Input the values shown in problems **c–k** on the *Absolute Value* activity sheet (page 112), and then complete the statements for problems **l–m**.

- Highlight the position in column *x*. Enter the absolute value number for *x*, e.g., –3. Press **ENTER**.

- Highlight the position in the **Y₁** column that is across from the number entered, and press **ENTER** again. The correct answer will appear.

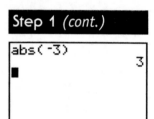

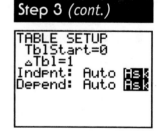

Conceptualizing Absolute Value *(cont.)*

Unit 2

Lesson 10

Using the Calculator *(cont.)*

Step 5 Graph the equations $y = x$ and $y = -x$.

- Press **ZOOM** and press **4** to select **ZDecimal**.
- Press **WINDOW** and changing **Xres** to **3**. This will make the calculator graph only every third pixel.

Step 6 Investigate the graph $y = |x|$.

- Press **Y=** and enter x into **Y₁** and $-x$ into **Y₂**. (Input x by pressing **X,T,θ,n**.)
- Have students use the left arrow to move the cursor to the left of the = sign and press **ENTER** until the dashed line appears.
- Press **GRAPH** and have students sketch the graph for problem **o** on the activity sheet, *Absolute Value* (page 113).
- Have them shade the portion of the graph of $y = x$ that represents the values of x for which $|x| = x$. Then, shade the portion of the graph of $y = -x$ that represents the values of x for which $|x| = -x$.

Step 7 Show the students how to shade portions of the graph on the calculator.

- On the graphing screen, select **DRAW** by pressing **2ND** followed by **PGRM**. Press **2** to select **Line**.
- The cursor should appear at the origin. Press **ENTER** to indicate the beginning of the line segment.
- Tell the students to use the arrows to drag a line across the upper portion of the graph of $y = x$. Press **ENTER** to finish the line.
- Use the arrows to return to the origin. Press **ENTER** to begin the line, and use the arrows to drag the line across the upper portion of $y = -x$. Press **ENTER** to end the line.

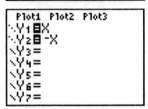

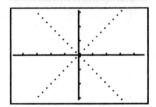

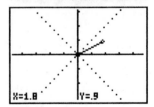

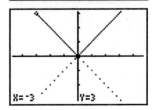

Conceptualizing Absolute Value *(cont.)*

Unit 2

Using the Calculator *(cont.)*

Step 8

Graph $y = |x|$ to show students that the graph of an absolute value is made up of pieces of the other two graphs.

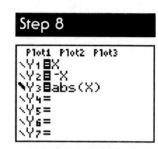

- Move the cursor next to Y₂. Press **ENTER** to select the thick line.

- Press **Y=** and enter **abs(x)** into Y₃. Insert **abs(** by pressing **MATH**, highlighting **NUM**, and pressing **1**.

- Press **X, T, Ø, n** for *x*. Press **)**. Press **GRAPH**.

Applying the Concept

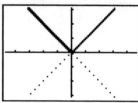

Step 1

Ask students the following questions to help them apply the concept of absolute value to real life.

- Why does the coordinate of the point give more information than its absolute value? *Emphasize that the coordinate indicates direction as well as magnitude.*

- How can the concept of a car traveling at 5 mph be interpreted in two different ways? *Answer: The car could be moving forward or backward.*

Step 2

Using the variable *t* for temperature, have students work with a partner to represent the following statements.

a. The temperature is two degrees above zero.

Answer: $t = 2$

b. The temperature is two degrees below zero.

Answer: $t = -2$

c. The temperature is two degrees from zero.

Answer: $t = |2|$

Conceptualizing Absolute Value *(cont.)*

Unit 2

Applying the Concept *(cont.)*

Step 3

Discuss the following statement:

The difference between Eliza's temperature and normal is 0.5°. Determine Eliza's possible temperatures.

- Help students write the statement $|98.6 - t| = .5$ to describe the relationship.

Step 4

Have the students complete the activity sheet, *Which Way Did They Go?* (page 114) to emphasize the meaning of absolute value.

Extension Ideas

- Show students that absolute value can be considered the *piecewise* function. Demonstrate the parts on the absolute value graph.

- Ask students what it means to say that your age must be within two years of sixteen and how this could be related to absolute value.

- Discuss why the statement $|x| = -4$ does not make sense.

Name _____

Date _____

Absolute Value

Directions: Plot the positions of the places chosen by your teacher on the number line below and complete the sentences.

School

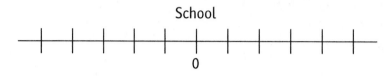

0

a. The _____ is _____ miles east of the school.

Its position could be indicated with the integer _____ .

b. The _____ is _____ miles west of the school.

Its position could be indicated with the integer _____ .

Directions: Complete the absolute value problems on the graphing calculator.

c. $|-3|$ = _____   **h.** $|5|$ = _____

d. $|-5|$ = _____   **i.** $|8|$ = _____

e. $|-8|$ = _____   **j.** $|4|$ = _____

f. $|-4|$ = _____   **k.** $|0|$ = _____

g. $|3|$= _____

l. To take the absolute value of a _____ number, take its opposite.

m. To take the absolute value of a _____ number, leave it the same.

Absolute Value *(cont.)*

n. Complete the table below. Check your answers on the calculator.

x	|x|
0	
−5	
7	
−3.4	
9.7	
−.001	
4,028	

o. Sketch the graphs of $y = x$ and $y = -x$ on the axes below. Shade the portion of the graph of $y = x$ that represents the values of x for which $x > 0$. Shade the portion of $y = -x$ that represents the values of x for which $x < 0$.

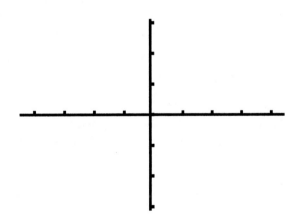

Name _____

Date _____

Which Way Did They Go?

Directions: On each of the number lines below, mark all of the numbers that have the indicated absolute value. Indicate the scale on each number line.

a. $|x| = 3$

0

b. $|x| = 20$

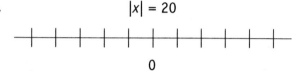

0

c. $|x| = 400$

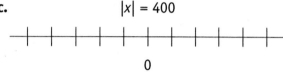

0

d. $|x| = .03$

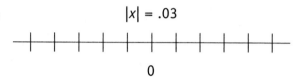

0

Directions: Write absolute value expressions to represent the scenarios below and give possible values to solve the problem.

e. Eileen is 15 years old. The difference between her age and Pablo's age is 5 years. What are Pablo's possible ages? Write an absolute value equation to describe the relationship.

f. Six months ago, Jason weighed 125 lbs. Since then, his weight has changed by 7 pounds. What are the possibilities for Jason's current weight? Write an absolute value equation to describe the relationship.

g. Mrs. Gonzalez measured the length of a wire and said that it was 10 cm $\pm$ .1. What is the greatest length the wire can be? What is its shortest possible length? Write an absolute value equation to describe the relationship.

Solving Absolute Value Equations and Inequalities

Unit 2

Lesson Description

- Students will solve equations and inequalities involving absolute values.

Materials

- *Absolutely!* (page 121; unt2.121.pdf)
- *Inside/Outside* (page 122; unt2.122.pdf)
- TI-83/84 Plus Family Graphing Calculator and TI-73 Explorer™

Explaining the Concept/Using the Calculator

Step 1

Review absolute value on the number line.

- Remind students that the solutions to $|x| = 5$ are all of the numbers on the x-axis that are 5 units from the origin, 5 and –5.

- Rewrite $|x| = 5$ as $|x – 0| = 5$ and point out that the zero represents the number from which the distance is measured.

- Ask the students to rewrite the statement, "All the numbers on the x-axis that are 11 units from 0.11." *Answer:* $|x – 11| = .11$

Step 2

Model how to solve equations in the form $|x – a| = b$. Have a student volunteer solve the following equation on the board.

$\|x – 1\| = 2$	
Greatest Value	**Least Value**
$x – 1 = 2$	$x – 1 = -2$
$x – 1 + 1 = 2 + 1$	$x – 1 + 1 = -2 + 1$
$x = 3$	$x = -1$

Step 3

Model how to solve the absolute value equations on the graphing calculator.

- Press [Y=]. Enter $|x – 1| = 2$ into Y_1.

- To enter the equation, access the absolute value command, **abs(**, in the catalog ([2ND], [0]).

- Press [X,T,θ,n] to insert *x*. Press [–], [1], and [)] to close the parentheses.

- Access = from the Test menu by pressing [2ND], [MATH], and then [1]. Then press [2].

- Choose the thick line graph by moving the cursor to the left of the first equal sign and pressing [ENTER] until it appears.

Step 3
Plot1 Plot2 Plot3
\Y₁▉abs(X–1)=2
\Y₂=
\Y₃=
\Y₄=
\Y₅=
\Y₆=
\Y₇=

Solving Absolute Value Equations and Inequalities *(cont.)*

Unit 2

Step 4

Explaining the Concept/Using the Calculator *(cont.)*

Have students graph the equation and analyze the solution.

Step 4

- Press ⬛ and then **4: ZDecimal** to graph the solution.

- Press ⬛ and ask the students to locate the solutions to the equations. Explain to students that the symbols in the Test menu produce *y*-values of 0, meaning false, or 1, meaning true.

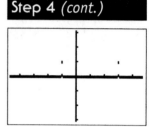

Step 4 *(cont.)*

- For problem **a** on *Absolutely!* (page 121), have the students record the solutions on the number line and find the number that is exactly halfway between them.

- Have students repeat the procedure for problem **b**, $|x + 1| = 2$, on *Absolutely!*.

Step 5

Have students work with a partner to find the solutions to the equation $|x - 3| = 10$. *Answer: −7 and 13*

- Taking this a step farther, have students determine the solutions to $|x + 3| = 10$. *Answer: 7 and −13*

- Ask students to explain what the solutions to the equations have in common. *Answer: Both are 10 and 13 units away from 3.*

Step 1

Using the Calculator

Have students graph the solutions to $|x + 3| = 10$.

Step 1

- Press ⬛. Enter **abs(*x* + 3)** into **Y₁** and **10** into **Y₂**. Refer to **Step 3** in the **Explaining the Concept/ Using the Calculator** section for how to access **abs(**.

- Press ⬛. Enter the settings below to view the complete graph of the absolute value equation and the area that intersects the horizontal line.

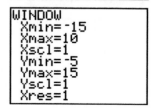

Step 1 *(cont.)*

  Xmin = −15, Xmax = 10, Xscl =1, Ymin = −5, Ymax = 15, Yscl = 1, Xres = 1

Solving Absolute Value Equations and Inequalities *(cont.)*

Unit 2

Using the Calculator *(cont.)*

Step 2 Have students find the intersection for the graph, using the intersect feature.

- Access **CALC** (**2ND** and then **TRACE**). Press **5** to select **intersect**.

Step 2

Step 3 Answer the prompts on the Graph screen to identify the intersection.

- For the prompt "**First curve?**" press **ENTER** to indicate the first line.

- The cursor will switch to the other line. The prompt "**Second curve?**" will appear. Press **ENTER** to indicate the second line.

- For the final prompt "**Guess?**," move the cursor close to the point of intersection.

- Press **ENTER** to display the coordinates of the point of intersection.

- This method locates points with the same *y*-values. The *y*-values are not actually part of the solution. The equation only involves the variable *x*.

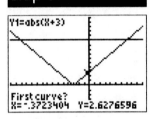

Step 3

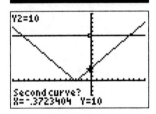

Step 3 *(cont.)*

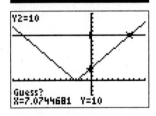

Step 3 *(cont.)*

Step 4 Have the students solve the equations for problems **c–e** on *Absolutely!* (page 121) by using the number lines.

- Discuss the example. Remind students that the center should be at 3 and the arrows should move 2 units to the right and left.

Step 5 Model how to solve absolute value compound inequalities with *greater than*, using **Example 2** from the activity sheet, *Absolutely!*.

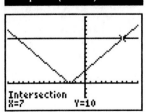

Step 3 *(cont.)*

$\|x - 1\| > 3$	
Greatest Value	**Least Value**
$x - 1 > 3$	$x - 1 < -3$
$x - 1 + 1 > 3 + 1$	$x - 1 + 1 < -3 + 1$
$x > 4$	$x < -2$

Solving Absolute Value Equations and Inequalities *(cont.)*

Unit 2

Using the Calculator *(cont.)*

Step 5

(cont.)

- Explain that the solution for $|x - 1| > 3$ consists of all the numbers that are more than 3 units away from −1.

- Explain that the *OR* means that the solution consists of any number on either part.

- Show students **Example 2** on *Absolutely!* (page 121).

Step 6 Show students how to check their answers graphically on the calculator.

- Press **Y=** and input **abs(x − 1)** for **Y₁** and **3** for **Y₂**.

- Shade above y = 3 and below |x − 1| to find the intersection. Highlight the correct graph style behind Y₁ and Y₂.

- Press **ZOOM** and then **6** to create a ZStandard window.

- Access **CALC** (**2ND** **TRACE**) and use **intersect** to find the range of values for *x*.

Step 7 Show the students how to check the solution using the Test menu and graphing.

- Press **Y=** . Enter **abs(x − 1) ≥ 3**. Input ≥ by pressing **2ND**, **MATH**, and then **4** .

- Press **GRAPH** and then **TRACE** . Use the right and left arrow keys to view the solutions.

- The Boolean Logic feature generates true (1) and false (0) values for *y*.

- The solution consists of the *x*-values where the *y*-value is 1.

- Have the students solve the inequality given in problem **f** on the activity sheet, *Absolutely!*.

Step 6
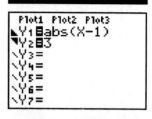

Step 6 *(cont.)*
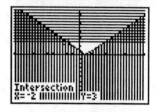

Step 6 *(cont.)*

Step 7

Step 7 *(cont.)*
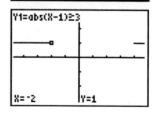

Solving Absolute Value Equations and Inequalities *(cont.)*

Unit 2

Using the Calculator *(cont.)*

Step 8

Model how to solve an absolute value inequality with *less than*. Use **Example 3** on *Absolutely!*.

$|x - 1| < 3$	
Greatest Value	**Least Value**
$x - 1 > -3$ $x - 1 + 1 > -3 + 1$ $x > -2$	$x - 1 < 3$ $x - 1 + 1 < 3 + 1$ $x < 4$

- Explain that the solution contains all numbers that are less than three units away from 1.
- Show the students how to solve the inequality using the number line on *Absolutely!* (page 121).

Step 9

Have students check their answers graphically by entering inequality **abs(*x* – 1)** into **Y₁** and **3** into **Y₂**.

- Have students shade below $y = 3$ to find the intersection. The solution consists of the *x*-values that appear in the shaded region.

Step 10

Have the students solve the inequality for **Example 3** on *Absolutely!*, using Boolean Logic.

- Students should check the solution using the Test menu and graphing.
- The solution consists of the *x*-values where the *y*-value is 1.
- Refer to **Step 7** for how to enter the equation, graph it, and determine the solution.

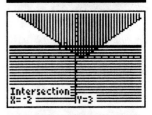

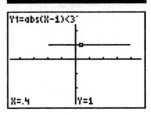

Solving Absolute Value Equations and Inequalities *(cont.)*

Unit 2

Applying the Concept

Step 1   Discuss situations where absolute value inequalities apply.

- Share with students the following scenario:

  If Jamila is 68 inches tall, write an inequality for all the students whose heights have more than a 5-inch difference from hers, $|h - 68| \geq 5$.

- Point out that this includes students who are taller or shorter than Jamila.

- Solve the inequality. Have the students who would be in this solution set stand up.

Step 2   Have students work with a partner to graph and solve the following scenario:

  McArnold's restaurant will only serve coffee when the temperature is within 3° of 158°. Point out that this is sometimes written as 158 ± 3.

- Help the students write the inequality $|t - 158| \leq 3$.

Step 3   Have students work in small groups to write their own absolute value inequality scenarios.

- Have small groups exchange scenarios with one another and solve each other's scenarios.

Step 4   Have students complete the *Inside/Outside* activity sheet (page 122).

Extensions

- Discuss situations in which *within an interval* and *outside an interval* are used. Have students relate these to absolute value.

- Have students look at other examples of compound inequalities.

- Have students investigate the use of tolerances in manufacturing and relate it to absolute value.

Name _____

Date _____

Absolutely!

Directions: Represent the solutions to the given equations on the number line and identify the number halfway between the solutions.

a. $|x - 1| = 2$

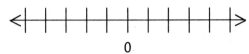

0

b. $|x + 1| = 2$

0

Directions: For each equation, locate the center point on the number line and draw points to represent the solutions. Check your solutions on the graphing calculator.

Example 1: $|x - 3| = 2$

0 1   5

Answer: Solutions are 1 and 5.

c. $|x - 2| = 3$

Solutions are _____.

d. $|x + 4| = 1$

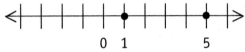

Solutions are _____.

e. $|x + 3| = 2$

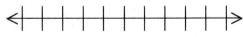

Solutions are _____.

Directions: Solve the inequalities on the number line.

Example 2: $|x - 1| > 3$

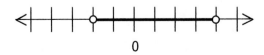

−2   0   4

Answer: The solution is x < −2 Or x > 4.

f. $|x + 2| > 3$

The solution is _____.

Example 3: $|x - 1| < 3$

0

Answer: The solution is −2 < x < 4.

g. $|x + 2| < 3$

The solution is _____.

Name _____

Date _____

Inside/Outside

Directions: Write and solve absolute value inequalities for each of the following. Use the number lines to help determine each solution and check your solution on the calculator.

a. Evelyn is trying to live on a budget. She has estimated $75 each month for clothing, but she expects to spend within $20 of the estimated amount. What are the actual limits of her budget?

_____

b. A game show contestant must guess the value of a boat within $1,000 to win it. The actual price of the boat is $15,248. What is the range of values within which he can guess and win the boat?

_____

c. The average height of the students in band class is 67 inches. There are no uniforms to fit students whose heights are more than 8 inches beyond that average. Describe the height of students whose uniforms will fit.

_____

d. The tolerance on the length of a bolt is .3 mm. If the bolt is supposed to be 42 mm long, describe the lengths of the bolts that must be rejected by quality control.

_____

Notes

Adding & Subtracting to Solve Systems of Equations

Unit 3

Lesson Description

- Students will solve a system of two linear equations with two variables using algebraically the addition and subtraction method and matrices.
- Students will apply algebraic techniques to solve rate problems, work problems, and percent mixture problems.

Materials

- *In the Mix!* (page 131; unt3.131.pdf)
- TI-83/84 Plus Family Graphing Calculator and TI-73 Explorer™

Explaining the Concept/Applying the Concept

Step 1

Ask students the following questions.

- What is a system? *Answers may vary.*
- What are some examples of systems? *Answers may vary, but may include the systems of the human body, a grading system, etc.*
- What is a system of equations? *Answer: A system of equations consists of two or more equations with two or more variables.*

Step 2

Model how to add and subtract a system of equations involving mixtures. Write the problem below on the board or overhead.

> *Your class sold 1,957 tickets to the football game. Adult tickets cost $3 each and student tickets cost $2 each. You took in a total of $5,035. How many student tickets and how many adult tickets did you sell?*

- Ask the students to pick a number of student tickets and find the number of adult tickets sold.
- Have them find the revenue for those numbers of tickets sold.
- Ask for a different number of student tickets, find the number of adult tickets, and the total revenue.
- Explain that there is only one pair that will give $5,035. That pair is the solution to the problem.

Adding & Subtracting to Solve Systems of Equations *(cont.)*
Unit 3

Explaining the Concept/Applying the Concept *(cont.)*

Step 3   Discuss characteristics of real-life systems of equations involving mixtures.

- Explain that this kind of problem, which involves the combining of items with different values, is called a mixture problem.
- Explain that the mixture method requires two equations, each involving the two totals in the problem.

Step 4   Model how to write two equations to represent the scenario in **Step 2**.

- Use x to represent the number of student tickets sold and y to represent the number of adult tickets sold.
- Have half the class work with partners to write an equation using x and y to represent the 1,957 tickets sold.
- Have the other half of the class work with partners to write an equation using x and y to represent the amount of money made in ticket sales, which is $5,035.
- Have students share their equations. Discuss why they are or are not representative of the problem.
- Show students the system of equations below:

$$x + y = 1,957$$

$$2x + 3y = 5,035$$

Step 5   Model how to solve the equation using linear combinations.

- Explain that a linear combination involves multiplying either (or both) equations by a number and adding or subtracting the new equations so that a variable is eliminated.

$$-2(x + y) = -2(1,957)$$
$$2x + 3y = 5,035$$
$$-2x - 2y = -3,914$$
$$\underline{2x + 3y = 5,035}$$
$$y = 1,121$$

Adding & Subtracting to Solve
Systems of Equations *(cont.)*

Unit 3

Step 5
(cont.)

Explaining the Concept/Applying the Concept *(cont.)*

Show that the other value can be found by eliminating the other variable.

$$\begin{cases} -3(x + y) = -3(1,957) \\ 2x + 3y = 5,035 \end{cases}$$

$$-3x - 3y = -5,871$$
$$\underline{\quad 2x + 3y = 5,035 \quad}$$
$$-x = -836$$
$$x = 836$$

- Ask students what the solutions 1,121 and 836 represent in the problem.

Using the Calculator

Step 1

Model how to enter the system of equations into the Matrix editor on the calculator.

- Explain to students that a matrix is a rectangular arrangement of values, and each value in the matrix is considered an element of the matrix.

- Explain that it is possible to use the Matrix editor on the graphing calculator to represent the coefficients of each equation. The coefficients are the elements of the matrix.

- Press **2ND** and then **x⁻¹** to access the **MATRIX** menu.

- Explain that the calculator has ten matrices, named **A** through **J**.

- Press the right arrow to highlight **EDIT**. This permits the user to change the existing matrices.

- Press **1** to select **[A]**.

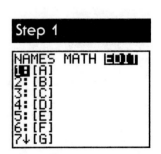

Step 2

Model how to edit the dimensions of the matrix.

- Explain that the first equation will be represented by a matrix with one row and three columns, which is a 1 x 3 matrix.

- Use the right arrows to highlight the dimensions to be edited and type over the number. For example, if a 1 x 1 matrix is set up, highlight the second **1** and press **3**. Then press **ENTER**.

Adding & Subtracting to Solve Systems of Equations *(cont.)*

Unit 3

Using the Calculator *(cont.)*

Step 3 Illustrate how to input the coefficients and constant terms for the first equation.

$$x + y = 1{,}957$$

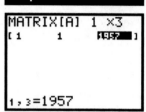

- The coefficients of the first equation representing the number of tickets sold are **1**, **1**, and **1,957**.

- Use the arrows to highlight the entries for the coefficients and constant terms of the first equation. Press **ENTER** after entering the new values for each entry.

  Moving from left to right, input the coefficients **1**, **1**, and **1,957**.

Step 4 Return to the Matrix editor. Enter the coefficients and constant terms to represent the second equation, which is the total amount earned from ticket sales.

$$2x + 3y = 5{,}035$$

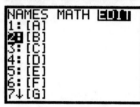

- Emphasize that it is necessary to return to the home screen by pressing **2ND** and then **MODE** before continuing.

- Press **2ND** and then **x⁻¹** to access the Matrix menu.

- Press the right arrow to highlight **EDIT**. Press ⟨ **2** ⟩ to select **[B]**.

- Set up a **1 x 3** matrix and enter the coefficients **2**, **3**, and **5,035**.

Step 5 Solve the system using the matrices.

- The two steps of eliminating variables can be accomplished with the matrices.

- Explain that the matrices can be combined, just like equations, so one of the first two entries is zero.

Step 6 Model how to paste a matrix to the Home screen.

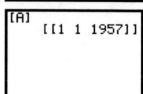

- Press **2ND** and then **MODE** to return to the Home screen.

- Press **2ND** and then **x⁻¹** to access the Matrix menu.

- Highlight **NAMES** and press ⟨ **1** ⟩ to select matrix **[A]**.

- Press **ENTER** to view the coefficients in matrix **[A]**.

Adding & Subtracting to Solve
Systems of Equations *(cont.)*

Unit 3

Using the Calculator *(cont.)*

Step 7

Model how to multiply all the entries in a matrix by –2.

- On the Home screen, press ((-)) and then (2).
- Access the Matrix menu. Highlight **NAMES** and select **1: [A]**.
- Press ENTER to multiply all three coefficients in the first equation by –2.

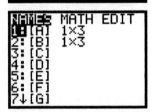

Step 8

Show how to solve the systems of equations for *y*. Multiply matrix **[A]** by –2 and add matrices **[A]** and **[B]** together.

- Return to the Home screen. Input **–2**.
- Access the Matrix menu. Highlight **NAMES** and select **1: [A]**.
- Input operation of addition by pressing (+).
- Access the Matrix menu. Highlight **NAMES** and select **2: [B]**.
- Press ENTER to execute the command.
- Notice a **0** represents the first coefficient of the variable *x* because that variable has been eliminated.
- A coefficient of **1** represents the variable *y*, indicating *y* is equal to 1,121.

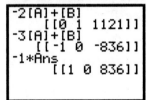

Step 9

Show students how to solve the system of equations for *x*. Multiply the matrix **[A]** by –3 and combine it with the second equation in matrix **[B]** to find the value of *x*.

- Repeat **Step 8**, except input **–3** in place of **–2**.
- Notice a 0 represents the second coefficient of the variable *y* because that variable has been cancelled out.
- A coefficient of **–1** represents the variable *x*, indicating –*x* is equal to –836.
- Multiply the result by –1. Press ((-)) and then (1) to input **–1**.
- Press 2ND and then ((-)) to recall the previous answer.
- Press ENTER to execute the command, *x* = 836.

Adding & Subtracting to Solve Systems of Equations *(cont.)*

Unit 3

Step 1

Applying the Concept

Write the following problem on the board and have students work in small groups to solve it using the addition and subtraction method:

Gabriella has $5,000 to invest. She deposits one amount into an account paying 3.5% simple interest and the rest into another account paying 4.5% simple interest. At the end of a year, she has earned a total of $190.78 in interest. How much did she invest in each account?

- Help students choose *x* as the variable for the amount in the first account and *y* as the amount in the second account.

- Help students identify the two totals, $5,000 and $190.78, and write equations involving *x* and *y* for each account.

$$x + y = 5,000$$
$$.045x + .035y = 190.78$$

Step 2

Have the class solve the problem using matrices on the graphing calculator.

- Help students determine coefficients and identify the dimensions of the matrices.

Step 3

Have groups present their solutions to the class in demonstrations on an overhead graphing calculator or using a projected TI-SmartView™. Or, have groups write out the steps for solving the problem on chart paper.

Step 4

Ask students the following question to assess their understanding of systems of equations and matrices: "How does solving systems of equations by hand translate to the matrices on the graphing calculator?" *Answers will vary.*

Step 5

Have the students complete the *In the Mix!* activity sheet (page 131).

Extension Ideas

- Have students write their own mixture problems.

- Have half the class solve the problem in the **Applying the Concept** section using the addition and subtraction method with matrices. Have the other half use the substitution method by entering the equations on the Y= screen, and graphing them as shown in Lesson 13 (pages 132–137).

In the Mix!

Directions: For each of the following problems, write a system of two equations using variables. Then, solve the system. Solve the problems with and without the graphing calculator.

a. Jamal was at the Candy and Cookies store at the mall to buy supplies for his school festival. Oatmeal cookies cost $4.00 per dozen and chocolate chip cookies cost $6 per dozen. Jamal spent $138 for 31 dozen cookies. How many of each kind of cookie did he buy?

b. Jamal also bought 158 brownies, some plain and some with frosting and nuts. The plain brownies cost $.75 a piece and the fancy ones cost $1.25 each. He spent $138.50 on brownies. How many of each kind did he purchase?

c. Elena was at the Paper for Parties store to buy plates, tableware, and table decorations. Large paper plates cost $2 for packs of 50 and small paper plates cost $1 for packs of 75. Elena spent $29 for a total of 1,275 plates. How many of each type of plate did she buy?

d. Plastic spoons cost $.06 apiece and forks cost $.07 each. Elena spent $47.50 on tableware. If she bought 733 pieces of tableware, how many spoons and how many forks did she buy?

Substituting to Solve Systems of Equations

Unit 3

Lesson Description

- Students solve a system of two linear equations in two variables algebraically and are able to interpret the answer graphically.
- Students use the substitution method to solve mixture problems.

Materials

- *Mixed Shirts* (page 138, unt3.138.pdf)
- TI-83/84 Plus Family Graphing Calculator and TI-73 Explorer™

Explaining the Concept/Applying the Concept

Step 1

Write the following mixture problem on the board and share it with the students.

Adrian has twice as many dimes as nickels. The total value of his money is $1.75. How many dimes and how many nickels does he have?

- Create a three-column chart with the headings, Number of Nickels, Number of Dimes, and Total Value.
- Have students estimate a possible number of nickels and dimes that may have the total value of $1.75. Record their estimations in the table. Then calculate the total value of their combinations.
- Explain that there is only one pair that will give $1.75. That pair is the solution to the problem.
- Explain that this kind of problem, involving the combination of items with different values, is called a *mixture problem*.

Step 2

Explain to students that a system of equations consists of two or more equations with two or more variables.

- Ask students how they would substitute an equation for a variable in another equation. Allow students to share their hypotheses.

Step 3

Have students write a system of equations representing the total number of dimes, *d*, and nickels, *n*, and the total value of the money.

$$d = 2n$$
$$.05n + .10d = 1.75$$

- Point out that it would be possible to write the number of nickels in terms of the number of dimes. Discuss if one way is easier than the other.
- Explain that by setting the first variable equal to the second variable, $2n$, can be substituted for the variable *d* in the second equation, leaving the second equation with only one variable.

$$.05n + .10(2n) = 1.75$$

Substituting to Solve Systems of Equations *(cont.)*

Unit 3

Explaining the Concept/Applying the Concept *(cont.)*

Step 4

Have the students solve the equation for *n* and then find *d*.

$$.5n + .20n = 1.75$$
$$.25n = 1.75$$
$$n = 7$$
$$d = 2(7)$$
$$d = 14$$

- Explain to the students that this method of solution is called *substitution* because an expression from one equation is being *substituted* into the other equation.

Using the Calculator

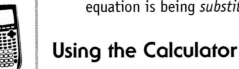

Step 1

Illustrate how to use the substitution method to solve the problem on the graphing calculator.

- Explain that the graphing calculator can enter equations only in terms of *x* and *y*.

- Have the students rewrite the nickel/dime equations in terms of *x* and *y* with *x* representing the number of nickels and *y* representing the number of dimes.

- Check the **MODE** by pressing [MODE] and the **FORMAT** by pressing [2ND] and then [ZOOM].

Step 2

Tell the students to enter the equations on the Y= screen.

- Press [Y=] to access the Y= screen.

- Clear any equations from Y= screen and turn off any Plots.

- By **Y₁**, input **2x**. Press [X,T,Ø,n] to insert *x*.

- By **Y₂**, input **.05x + .10Y₁**. To insert **Y₁**, press [VARS], highlight **Y-VARS**, press [1] to select **Function**, and press [1] to select **Y₁**. By **Y₃**, input **1.75.**

- Turn **Y₁** off by using the left arrow to highlight the = and press [ENTER]. **Y₁** will not graph because the = is not highlighted.

- By replacing the *y* in the second equation with Y₁, the expression for dimes has been substituted into Y₂.

Step 1 *(cont.)*

Step 2

Step 2 *(cont.)*

Step 2 *(cont.)*

Substituting to Solve Systems of Equations *(cont.)*

Unit 3

Using the Calculator *(cont.)*

Step 3

Help the students set up an accomodating window to display these equations.

Step 3

- Press **WINDOW** and input the settings shown in the screen shot to the right. Move the cursor next to window variables to enter a value.

- Explain that **Ymax** is the largest value on the *y*-axis and therefore, should be a little larger than 1.75.

- Explain that **Xmax** is the largest value for the *x*-axis. Ask students what is the largest number of coins that could yield 1.75 to determine a good choice for **Xmax**.

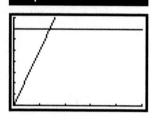

Step 4

Step 4

Model how to graph the equations and determine the intersection.

- Press **GRAPH**. In this case, the Trace feature can't be used to determine the intersection.

- Access the **CALC** to find the intersection of the two lines by pressing **2ND** and then **TRACE**. Press [**5**] to select **intersect**.

Step 4 *(cont.)*

- The question **First curve?** will appear on the screen. Press **ENTER** to select the first line.

- The question **Second curve?** will appear on the screen. Press **ENTER** to select the second line.

- The question **Guess?** will appear on the screen. Use the right/left arrows to move the cursor close to the point of intersection, and press **ENTER**.

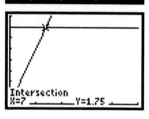

Step 4 *(cont.)*

- The intersection will be given as $x = 7$ and $y = 1.75$.

Step 5

Ask students the following questions about the graph and intersection.

- Which coordinates represents nickels?
  Answer: x represents the total number of nickels.

- How do you find the number of dimes?
  Answer: Substitute in the number of nickels for x in the first equation.

Substituting to Solve Systems of Equations *(cont.)*

Unit 3

Using the Calculator *(cont.)*

Step 6 Show the students how to use the graphing calculator to find the number of dimes.

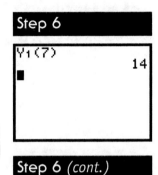

Step 6

$Y_1(7)$

14

- Return to the Home screen by pressing **2ND** and then **MODE**.

- Input $Y_1(7)$. Access Y_1 by pressing **VARS**, highlighting **Y-VARS**, press (1) to select **Function**, and press (1) to select Y_1.

- Insert (7), by pressing **(**, (7), and then **)**.

- Press **ENTER** to execute the command.

Step 7 Point out that the previous problem was easily solved using substitution because one of the variables was expressed in terms of the other (twice as many dimes as nickels).

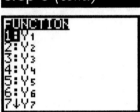

Step 6 *(cont.)*

FUNCTION
1:Y1
2:Y2
3:Y3
4:Y4
5:Y5
6:Y6
7↓Y7

- Explain that substitution works well if one of the variables can be expressed in the form kx or $x + k$.

Explaining the Concept/Using the Calculator

Step 1 Have students solve the following problem:

Elena has $9,000 invested in two different funds, one offering 5% annual interest and the other offering 6% annual interest. At the end of the year, she had earned $510 in interest. How much did she have invested in each fund?

- Use x for the amount in the first fund and y for the amount in the second fund.

Step 2 Ask students if one of these variables can be easily written in terms of the other.

- Point out that it is possible to write either $y = 9,000 - x$ or $x = 9,000 - y$. Both will yield the solution.

Step 3 Have students work with a partner to write the equation for the total amount of interest.

$$.05x + .06y = 510$$

Explaining the Concept/Using the Calculator *(cont.)*

Step 4   Have students use substitution to solve the system.

$$\begin{cases} y = 9{,}000 - x \\ .05x + .06y = 510 \end{cases}$$

$$.05x + .06(9{,}000 - x) = 510$$

$$.05x + 540 - .06x = 510$$

$$-.01x = -30$$

$$x = 3{,}000$$

$$y = 9{,}000 - 3{,}000$$

$$y = 6{,}000$$

Step 5   Have students use substitution on the graphing calculator to solve the problem.

- Refer to the **Using the Calculator** section, **Steps 2–4** for specific keystrokes.

- First enter the equations on the Y= screen. Then graph those equations.

- Be sure to create an appropriate window for the range of values being graphed.

- Finally, use the intersect feature on the Calc menu to find *x*.

Step 5

```
Plot1 Plot2 Plot3
\Y1=9000-X
\Y2￼.05X+.06Y1
\Y3￼510
\Y4=
\Y5=
\Y6=
\Y7=
```

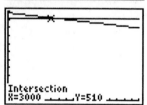

Step 5 *(cont.)*

```
Intersection
X=3000          Y=510
```

Step 6   Ask students why substitution would be difficult to use to solve the following system. *Answer: In both equations, the variables are written in terms of the other because all variables have a coefficient greater than one and the coefficients are not divisible by one another.*

$$\begin{cases} 3x + 2y = 10 \\ 2x + 5y = 3 \end{cases}$$

Applying the Concept

Step 1   Show students a system whose solution does not make sense. Share the following problem with students.

Cynthia has $2,000 invested in two accounts, one at 2% annual interest and the other at 3% annual interest. At the end of the year, she has $80 in interest. How much does she have in each account?

Substituting to Solve Systems of Equations *(cont.)*

Lesson 13

Unit 3

Step 2

Applying the Concept *(cont.)*

Have the students work in small groups to solve the system, as shown below.

$$\begin{cases} y = 2{,}000 - x \\ .03x + .02y = 80 \end{cases}$$

- Have half the groups solve the problem, using the calculator. Have the other half solve the problem using pencil and paper. Have students present their solutions.

$$.03x + .02(2{,}000 - x) = 80$$
$$.03x + 40 - .02x = 80$$
$$.01x = 40$$
$$x = 4{,}000$$

- Ask the students why the solution does not make sense. *Answer: x is greater than the amount invested.*

Step 3

Show the students a system that has no solution.

- Ask the students to work in small groups to solve the system below.

$$\begin{cases} y = 2{,}000 - x \\ x + y = 80 \end{cases}$$

- Tell the students that an impossible statement means there is no solution.

$$x + (2{,}000 - x) = 80$$
$$2{,}000 = 80$$

Step 4

Have the students complete the *Mixed Shirts* activity sheet (page 138).

Extension Idea

- Have students work with a partner to respond to the following question. How does solving systems of equation using substitution by hand translate to the graphing calculator? *Answers may vary.*

Name _____

Date _____

Mixed Shirts

Directions: For each of the following problems, choose variables and write a system of two equations. Then, solve the system with and without the graphing calculator.

Desmond has a weekend job selling T-shirts at a booth at the flea market. Small, medium, and large sizes cost $12. Extra-large (XL) and extra-extra-large (XXL) shirts cost $14.

a. In one weekend, Desmond sold 240 shirts and took in $2,964. How many XL and XXL shirts did he sell?

b. The following weekend, Joe got his bookkeeping mixed up. He took in $6,000 but thought he sold 400 shirts. Use a system of equations to show how Joe was wrong.

c. On a third weekend, Joe sold only XL and large shirts. He sold 5 times as many XL shirts as small shirts. He took in $984. How many of each did he sell?

d. On the last weekend, Joe sold only XL and large shirts. He sold 25 more XL shirts than he did large shirts. He took in $2,742. How many of each did he sell?

Using Inverse Matrices to Solve Systems of Equations

Unit 3

Lesson Description
- Students will solve systems of linear equations with two variables using inverse matrices.
- Students will understand the concept of an inverse matrix.

Materials
- *Just Nutty!* (pages 146–147; unt3.146.pdf)
- *A New Dimension* (page 148; unt3.148.pdf)
- TI-83/84 Plus Family Graphing Calculator or TI-73 Explorer™

Explaining the Concept

Step 1   Ask students the following questions.
- What is a matrix? *Answer: A rectangular arrangement of values*
- What are the elements of a matrix? *Answer: The values*

Step 2   Explain that a system of linear equations such as the one shown below can be represented in the form $ax = b$.

$$\begin{cases} x + 2y = 5 \\ 3x + 5y = 14 \end{cases}$$

Step 3   Explain how to set up matrices representing a system of equations in $ax = b$ form.
- Line up the values of x, y, and the constants values.

$$\begin{cases} x + 2y = 5 \\ 3x + 5y = 14 \end{cases}$$

- Write the values in the equations as equivalent matrices.

$$\begin{bmatrix} 1x \\ 3x \end{bmatrix} \begin{bmatrix} 2y \\ 5y \end{bmatrix} = \begin{bmatrix} 5 \\ 14 \end{bmatrix}$$

- Separate the variables from the coefficients.

$$\begin{bmatrix} 1 & 2 \\ 3 & 5 \end{bmatrix} \bullet \begin{bmatrix} x \\ y \end{bmatrix} = \begin{bmatrix} 5 \\ 14 \end{bmatrix}$$

- Enter the numerical matrices in the graphing calculator. Matrix [A] will represent the coefficients of the variables. Matrix [B] will represent the constants.

Using Inverse Matrices to Solve Systems of Equations *(cont.)*

Unit 3

Using the Calculator

Step 1

Have students set up Matrix [A] on the graphing calculator.

- Press **2ND** followed by **x⁻¹** to access **MATRIX**.
- Explain that the calculator has ten matrices, named **A** through **J**.
- Press the right arrow to highlight **EDIT**. This allows the user to change the existing matrices.
- Press **1** to select Matrix [**A**].
- Explain that the coefficients will be represented with a 2 x 2 matrix (two rows and two columns).
- To change the dimensions of the matrix to **2 x 2**, highlight the dimension to be edited and type over the number. Then press **ENTER**.

Step 2

Explain how to input the coefficients for the variables into Matrix [A].

- Enter the coefficients for both equations in Matrix [A] by highlighting the entry, typing the number, and pressing **ENTER**.
- Press **1**, **2**, **3**, **5** to set up the matrix as shown below.

$$A = \begin{bmatrix} 1 & 2 \\ 3 & 5 \end{bmatrix}$$

Step 3

Explain how to input the constant terms into Matrix [B].

- Return to the Home screen by pressing **2ND** and then **MODE**, before continuing.
- Press **2ND** and then **x⁻¹** to return to the Matrix editor.
- Highlight **EDIT**. Press **2** to select Matrix [**B**].
- Set up a 2 x 1 matrix (two rows and one column).
- Input that the constants shown below by highlighting the entry, typing the numbers, and then pressing **ENTER**.

$$B = \begin{bmatrix} 5 \\ 14 \end{bmatrix}$$

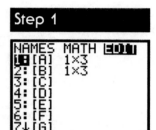

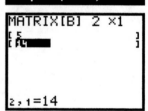

Using Inverse Matrices to Solve a System of Equations *(cont.)*

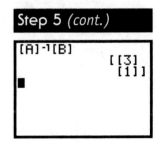

Unit 3

Step 4

Using the Calculator *(cont.)*

Explain to students that the matrix equation can be solved in a way that is similar to solving the linear equation $ax = b$.

- To solve, divide each side by a.

$$\frac{ax}{a} = \frac{b}{a}$$

- This is equivalent to multiplying both sides of the equation by the multiplicative inverse.

$$\frac{b}{a} = a^{-1}b.$$

- Explain that on the graphing calculator the solution is obtained by multiplying the inverse of the coefficients of the variables by the constants.

$$\begin{bmatrix} x \\ y \end{bmatrix} = \begin{bmatrix} 1 & 2 \\ 3 & 5 \end{bmatrix}^{-1} \begin{bmatrix} 5 \\ 14 \end{bmatrix}$$

- Explain that the solution $x = a^{-1}b$ will be inputted into the graphing calculator to represent the above operation.

Step 5

Show students on the graphing calculator how to multiply the inverse of matrix A by matrix B to find the values for x.

- Press **2ND** and then **MODE** to return to the Home screen.

- Enter **A⁻¹B** on the Home screen by pressing **2ND** and then **x⁻¹** to access the Matrix menu. Highlight **NAMES**.

- Press **1** to select **[A]**. Press **x⁻¹** to insert the inverse command.

- Repeat the steps above, but press **2** to insert the **[B]**.

- Press **ENTER** to execute the command.

- The top number in the matrix is the value for x and the lower number is y.

Using Inverse Matrices to Solve a System of Equations *(cont.)*

Unit 3

Using the Calculator *(cont.)*

Step 6   Show students how to check the solution by graphing.

- Have the students solve each of the equations in the system for *y*.

$$x + 2y = 5$$
$$y = \frac{5 - x}{2}$$
$$3x + 5y = 14$$
$$y = \frac{14 - 3x}{5}$$

- Check **MODE** and **FORMAT** (`2ND`, `ZOOM`) settings to ensure all left-hand settings are selected.

Step 7   Have students enter the equations in the system on the Y= screen.

- Press `Y=`. Clear any equations from the Y= screen and turn off any Plots.

- By **Y₁**, input **(5 − x)/2**. By **Y₂**, input **(14 −3x)/5**. To insert *x*, press `X,T,θ,n`.

- Remind the students to use parentheses around the numerators of the fractions.

Step 8   Model how to set up an accomodating window.

- Press `ZOOM` and then `6` to select **ZStandard**.

Step 9   Have students find the point of intersection of the lines.

- Access **CALC** by pressing `2ND` and then `TRACE`.

- Press `5` to select **intersect**.

- Answer the question, **First curve?,** by pressing `ENTER` to select the first line.

- Answer the question, **Second curve?,** by pressing `ENTER` to select the second line.

- Answer the question, **Guess?,** by using the right/ left arrows to move the cursor close to the point of intersection and then pressing `ENTER`.

Step 7

Step 8

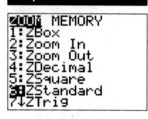

Step 8 *(cont.)*

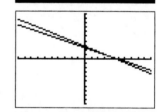

Step 9

Step 9 *(cont.)*

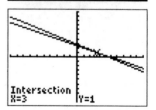

Using Inverse Matrices to Solve a System of Equations *(cont.)*

Unit 3

Step 10

Using the Calculator *(cont.)*

Have students work with a partner to solve the following problem using inverse matrices.

$$\begin{cases} .08x + .076y = 703.80 \\ x + y = 9000 \end{cases}$$

- Ask the students to identify the coefficient and constant matrices and enter them into [**A**] and [**B**] on the graphing calculator.

- Ask the students how to solve the matrix equation and have them solve it on their calculators.

- If they want the answers rounded, have them select **MODE**, to change the decimal to two places by highlighting **2** and pressing **ENTER**.

- Return to the Home screen and select **ANS** by pressing **2ND** followed by the **(-)**. Press **ENTER**.

- Remind the students to return the Mode settings to the defaults.

Step 1

Applying the Concept

Have students write a system of three equations with three variables to represent problem ***a*** on the *Just Nutty!* activity sheet (page 146). It is also provided below. Then create matrices on the graphing calculator.

You want to prepare 9 pounds of a snack mix. You plan to buy almonds for $2.45 per pound, peanuts for $1.85 per pound, and raisins for $.80 per pound. You have $15 and you want the total weight of the nuts to be twice the weight of the raisins. How much of each ingredient should you purchase?

***Optional*—Steps 3** and **4** introduce how to solve the system of three equations by hand. This may be too difficult for many Algebra I students, but it may serve as a way to differentiate the lesson for more advanced students.

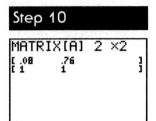

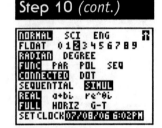

Applying the Concept *(cont.)*

Step 2

Write an equation for the total pounds of ingredients, for the cost of the mixture, and for the weight of the raisins and the nuts.

Scenarios	Equation
Total Pounds of Ingredients	$a + p + r = 9$
Cost of the Mixture	$2.45a + 1.85p + .80r = 15$
Weight of the Raisins and the Nuts	$a + p = 2r$

Step 3

Model the following steps to solve the system of equations.

- Solve the third equation, representing the weight of ingredients for a.

$$a = 2r - p$$

Step 4

Then substitute the third equation for a in the first and second equation. Then, solve the first equation followed by the second equation.

Equation 1: Total Pounds of Ingredients	Equation 2: Cost of Mixture
• **Write the equation.** $a + p + r = 9$ • **Substitute for a.** $(2r - p) + p + r = 9$ • **Combine like terms.** $2r + r - p + p = 9$ • **Solve for r.** $3r = 9$ $r = 3$	$2.45a + 1.85p + .80r = 15$ • **Substitute for a.** $2.45(2r - p) + 1.85p + .80r = 15$ • **Substitute for r.** $2.45(2 \cdot 3 - p) + 1.85p + .80 \cdot 3 = 15$ • **Multiply.** $2.45(6 - p) + 1.85p + 2.40 = 15$ • **Distribute.** $14.70 + 2.40 - 2.45p + 1.85p = 15$ • **Combine like Terms.** $17.10 - .60p = 15$ • **Arrange in $ax + b$ form.** $17.10 - .60p = 15$ $-15 + .60p = -15 + .60p$ $2.10 = .60p$ • **Divide both sides by $.60p$.** $2.10/.60 = .60/p$ $3.50 = p$

Using Inverse Matrices to Solve a System of Equations *(cont.)*

Unit 3

Applying the Concept *(cont.)*

Step 5 Model how to substitute the known values to solve the problem by asking students the following questions.

- What is the problem asking? *Answer: How many pounds of each ingredient you should purchase.*

- In which equation should the values be substituted to solve the problem? *Answer: a + p + r = 9*

$$a + 3.5 + 3 = 9$$

$$a + 6.5 = 9$$

$$-6.5 = -6.5$$

$$a = 2.5$$

Step 6 Ask the students how to write the coefficient and constant matrices to represent the three equations.

- Have the students identify the dimensions and values of the 3 x 3 coefficient matrix and the 3 x 1 constants matrix.

$$a = \begin{bmatrix} 1 & 1 & 1 \\ 2.45 & 1.85 & .80 \\ 1 & 1 & -2 \end{bmatrix} \qquad b = \begin{bmatrix} 9 \\ 15 \\ 0 \end{bmatrix}$$

- Tell the students to enter the matrices into their calculators and solve the system. Students should enter **[A]⁻¹[B]**.

- Have the students check the solutions in the equations.

- Ask the students to express the solution to the word problem in sentence form and have students present the solution to the system.

Step 7 Have the students complete the activity sheet *A New Dimension* (page 148).

Extension Ideas

- Have students complete the **Try it on your own!** section on the activity sheet, *Just Nutty!* (page 147).

- Have small groups present a solution to one of the problems on *A New Dimension* (page 148). On one half of the paper, students should record the steps for solving the equation by hand. On the other half of the paper, students should record the steps for solving the equation on the graphing calculator.

- Have students write their own three-variable system of equation problems.

Name _____

Date _____

Just Nutty!

Directions: Solve the problem, using a system of three equations with three variables.

You want to prepare 9 pounds of a snack mix. You plan to buy almonds for $2.45 per pound, peanuts for $1.85 per pound, and raisins for $.80 per pound. You have $15 and you want the total weight of the nuts to be twice the weight of the raisins. How much of each ingredient should you purchase?

a. Write an equation to represent each scenario.

Scenarios	Equation
Total Pounds of Ingredients	
Cost of the Mixture	
Weight of the Raisins and the Nuts	

b. Solve the third equation for a.

c. Use the hints given in the table to complete the steps to solve for r and p.

Equation 1: Total Pounds of Ingredients	Equation 2: Cost of Mixture
• **Substitute for a.**	• **Substitute for a.**
	• **Substitute for r.**
• **Combine like terms.**	• **Multiply.**
	• **Distribute.**
• **Solve for r.**	• **Combine like terms.**
	• **Solve for p.**

d. Substitute the values above to solve the problem. Show your work.

Just Nutty! *(cont.)*

Directions: Solve the problem above using matrices on the graphing calculator.

e. Record the matrices entered into the graphing calculator and label the dimensions of the matrix.

$$\begin{bmatrix} \text{Coefficients} \\[12pt] \text{Dimensions:} \end{bmatrix} \quad \begin{bmatrix} \text{Constants} \\[12pt] \text{Dimensions:} \end{bmatrix}$$

f. Record the expression entered into the Home screen to solve the system of equations.

_____

g. Record the solution given in the matrices and explain the solution in sentence form.

_____

_____

Try it on your own!

Hannah's mother has $6,000 dollars to invest in three different banks. The First National Bank offers 5% interest, the Second City Bank offers 4%, and the Great State Bank offers 3.5%. She wants to invest twice as much in the First National Bank as in the Great State Bank, and hopes to earn $255 interest in a year. How much should she invest in each bank?

h. Write a system of three equations and record it below.

_____

i. Record the expression entered into the Home screen to solve the system of equations.

_____

j. Record the solution given in the matrices and explain the solution in sentence form.

_____

_____

Name _____

Date _____

A New Dimension

Directions: Solve the systems of equations using inverse matrices. If necessary, rearrange the equations to form the matrices. Check the solutions of systems with two equations by graphing. Check the solutions of systems by substituting the values into the equations.

a. $\begin{cases} 4x + 3y = 31 \\ 2x - y = -7 \end{cases}$

b. $\begin{cases} x + 2y = 1 \\ 5x - 4y = -23 \end{cases}$

c. $\begin{cases} 4x + y = 5 \\ y = 2x + 2 \end{cases}$

d. $\begin{cases} -3x + y = 4 \\ -9x + 5y = 10 \end{cases}$

e. $\begin{cases} 3x - 5y + z = 9 \\ x - 3y - 2z = -8 \\ 5x - 6y + 3z = 15 \end{cases}$

f. $\begin{cases} x - 3z = 7 \\ 2x + y - 2z = 11 \\ -x - 2y + 2z = -15 \end{cases}$

Unit 4

Investigating Roots & Fractional Exponents

Unit 4

Lesson Description

- Students will understand the inverse relationship of raising to a power and extracting the root of a perfect square integer. For an integer that is not square, students will determine the two integers between which its square root lies and explain why.

- Students will understand and use taking a root and raising to a fractional power. Students will know the laws of fractional exponents. Students will apply the use of roots to real-life situations.

Materials

- *Growing Roots* (pages 155–156; unt4.155.pdf)
- *Fractional Exponents* (pages 157–158; unt4.157.pdf)
- *Math Carnival* (page 159; unt4.159.pdf)
- TI-83/84 Plus Family Graphing Calculator or TI-73 Explorer™

Using the Calculator

Step 1 Ask the students, "What is the meaning of *square root?*" *Answer: When the product of two identical factors is a second number, the factor is the square root.*

- Many students will be able to give the answer to the question, "What is the square root of nine?," but will be unable to explain why.

Step 2 Ask the students to enter 3^2 on their calculators.

- There are two ways to enter this. Either press ⟨ 3 ⟩ and then ▮ x^2 ▮. Or press ⟨ 3 ⟩, ▮ ^ ▮, and then ⟨ 2 ⟩.

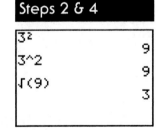

Step 3 Draw the diagram below on the board. Explain that the symbol is called a radical and the number under the *radical* is called the *argument of the expression*.

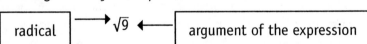

| radical | → $\sqrt{9}$ ← | argument of the expression |

Special Note: It is a good idea to use closing parentheses in preparation for more complicated expressions, even though it is not needed for simple expressions.

Step 4 Have students calculate the square root of nine, $\sqrt{9}$, on the graphing calculator.

Press ▮ 2ND ▮ and then ▮ x^2 ▮ to access the square root symbol.

- Press ⟨ 9 ⟩ after the parenthesis and press ▮) ▮ to close parentheses. Press ▮ ENTER ▮ to execute the command.

Investigating Roots & Fractional Exponents *(cont.)*

Unit 4

Explaining the Concept

Step 1

On the activity sheet, *Growing Roots* (page 155), have students write mathematical statements and then the sentence describing the relationship between the square of the number and the square root of the answer.

- For statements **a–b** on the activity sheet, *Growing Roots*, have students write the two mathematical statements, $3^2 = 9$ and $\sqrt{9} = 3$.

- Then for statement **c**, students should write "The square root of 9 is 3 because $3^2 = 9$."

- For statement **d**, have a student volunteer to select another number larger than 15. Have the students square the number and then take the square root of the answer on the calculator. Students should record the expressions.

- For statement **e**, have the students write an expression for numbers larger than one.

Step 2

Have the students repeat the steps above with numbers between zero and one. Students should complete the statements for **f–g** on the activity sheet, *Growing Roots*.

- Explain that the graphing calculator will switch to scientific notation when there is a large number of decimal places.

- For example, if the statement 9E-6 appears, it means 9×10^{-6} or .000009. *E* represents the base, 10, and –6 represents the number of zeros.

- Have students draw some conclusions about irrational numbers. Have students answer the question, "What is an irrational number?" for question **h** on the activity sheet, *Growing Roots*. *Answer: If a whole number is not a perfect square it is an irrational number, meaning it cannot be represented as a ratio of integers.*

Step 3

Have students work with a partner to develop a statement that generalizes how to predict whether the square root of a number will be larger or smaller than the number. *Answer: If the number is between zero and one, the square root will be larger. If the number is greater than one, the square root will be smaller.*

- Students should record their answers for question **i** on the activity sheet, *Growing Roots*.

Investigating Roots & Fractional Exponents *(cont.)*

Unit 4

Using the Calculator

Step 1

Have the students enter 2^3 on the calculator.

- Remind them that the cube symbol can be entered either by pressing **^** and then **3**, or by pressing **MATH** and choosing **3: ^{3}**.

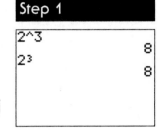

Step 1

```
2^3
                    8
2³
                    8
```

Step 2

Have students complete the statement for $2^3 = 8$ by letter **j** on the activity sheet, *Growing Roots* (page 156).

- Ask students what it means to cube a number. *Answer: Multiplying the same number three times, or the product of three equal factors.*

- Ask them what the inverse operation is of cubing a number. *Answer: Calculating the cube root*

- Show students how to write $\sqrt[3]{8}$. Explain that the three is called the root index.

- Ask the students what the root index would be for square roots. *Answer: Explain that it is omitted because the square root is the most frequently used root.*

Step 3

Have the students complete expressions, similar to the ones they wrote for the square roots for **k–l** on the *Growing Roots* activity sheet.

Step 4

Explain roots of orders higher than a cube and show students how to enter them in the graphing calculator.

- Have students calculate $\sqrt[5]{32}$.

- Explain that the syntax on the calculator requires the root index, the radical, and then the argument.

- On the Home screen, press **5** for the root index.

- Press **MATH** and then **5** to paste the symbol, $\sqrt[x]{\ }$, to the Home screen.

- Press **3**, **2** to enter the arguement.

- Press **ENTER** to execute the command.

Step 4

```
5ˣ√32
                    2
```

Step 4 *(cont.)*

```
MATH NUM CPX PRB
1:▶Frac
2:▶Dec
3:³
4:³√(
5:ˣ√
6:fMin(
7↓fMax(
```

Step 5

Have students write mathematical statements describing the relationship for powers and their roots greater than a cube for **m–n** on the *Growing Roots* activity sheet.

Investigating Roots & Fractional Exponents *(cont.)*

Unit 4

Using the Calculator *(cont.)*

Step 6

Ask the students to calculate $\sqrt{47}$, $\sqrt{75}$, $\sqrt{2,401}$. Students should record their answers by **o–q** on the *Growing Roots* activity sheet (page 156).

- Ask them why the first two have so many decimal places and the last one does not. Have students record their answers for question **p** on the activity sheet.

- When students check an answer on the calculator by squaring it, it seems as though the decimals are exact.

- Explain to students that the decimals are not exact; the calculator rounds the irrational numbers.

- Point out that there is no repeating pattern for roots that do not come out even. These roots are one-of-a kind irrational numbers. Look at other irrational numbers from roots of higher orders.

Applying the Concept

Step 1

Have students complete the *Fractional Exponents* activity sheet (pages 157–158) in small groups. Be sure to have the class come to an agreement on the answers.

Step 2

Model the following problem for students. Then, assign different groups of students problems from the *Math Carnival* activity sheet (page 159). Have each group present their solutions to the class.

Bob has volunteered to wear a costume to entertain the children at the carnival. It will look like a sponge in the shape of a cube. You plan to build a frame and cover the top and sides of it with a sponge like material that is 2 inches thick. (You'll cut a hole for Bob's head to go through when you finish.) To fit Bob, each side of the cube must be wider than his shoulder width. You have a large piece of the material that you plan to cut up to use for Bob's costume. The volume of the material is 4,529 cubic inches. What is the largest width for Bob's shoulders that will fit into the costume?

$$v = 5 \bullet 2 \bullet w^2$$
$$4,529 = 10w^2$$
$$452.9 = w^2$$
$$\sqrt{452.9} = w$$
$$21.28 \approx w$$

Answer: Bob's shoulders can be no wider than 21.28 inches.

Extension Idea

- Have students select various positive and negative numbers to calculate their cube roots. Ask students to write a statement about whether the cube root of integers are negative or positive. *Answer: The cube root of a positive number is always positive. The cube root of a negative number is always negative.*

Name _____

Date _____

Growing Roots

Directions: Write mathematical statements and then the sentence describing the relationship between the square of the number and the square root of the answer.

a. square of three

_____ = _____

b. square root of 9

_____ = _____

c. The square root of _____ is _____ because _____ = _____.

Directions: For statement **d**, complete the expressions using a number larger than 15. For statement **e**, use a number larger than one. For statements **f–g**, use numbers between zero and one.

d. square of _____   square root of _____

_____ = _____   _____ = _____

The square root of _____ is _____ because _____ = _____.

e. square of _____   square root of _____

_____ = _____   _____ = _____

The square root of _____ is _____ because _____ = _____.

f. square of _____   square root of _____

_____ = _____   _____ = _____

The square root of _____ is _____ because _____ = _____.

g. square of _____   square root of _____

_____ = _____   _____ = _____

The square root of _____ is _____ because _____ = _____.

h. What is an irrational number?

_____

_____

Growing Roots *(cont.)*

i. Make a statement generalizing how you can predict whether the square root of a number will be larger or smaller than the number.

_____

_____

Directions: Write mathematical statements and then complete the sentence describing the relationship between the cube of the number and the cube root of the answer.

j. cube of two   cube root of 8

_____ = _____   _____ = _____

The cube root of _____ is _____ because _____ = _____.

k. cube of _____   cube root of _____

_____ = _____   _____ = _____

The cube root of _____ is _____ because _____ = _____.

l. cube of _____   cube root of _____

_____ = _____   _____ = _____

The cube root of _____ is _____ because _____ = _____.

Directions: Write mathematical statements describing the relationship for powers and their roots greater than a cube. For example, 2 is the fifth root of 32 because 2 to the fifth power is equal to 32.

m. _____

n. _____

Directions: Calculate the following. Then answer the question below about your results.

o. $\sqrt{47}$ = _____

p. $\sqrt{75}$ = _____

q. $\sqrt{2401}$ = _____

r. Why do the first two have so many decimal places and the last one does not?

_____

_____

Name _____

Date _____

Fractional Exponents

Directions: Follow the steps below and answer the questions.

a. Use your graphing calculator to complete the chart below.

	2^{nth}	Square Root		3^{nth}	Square Root		5^{nth}	Square Root
a	$2^8 =$	$\sqrt{a} =$		$3^8 =$	$\sqrt{a} =$		5^8	$\sqrt{a} =$
b	$2^4 =$	$\sqrt{b} =$		$3^4 =$	$\sqrt{b} =$		5^4	$\sqrt{b} =$
c	$2^2 =$	$\sqrt{c} =$		$3^2 =$	$\sqrt{c} =$		5^2	$\sqrt{c} =$
d	$2^1 =$	$\sqrt{d} =$		$3^1 =$	$\sqrt{d} =$		5^1	$\sqrt{d} =$

b. Look at the exponents in each of the columns. What is the relationship between each exponent and the one above it?

_____

_____

c. What was the effect on the number when the exponent was multiplied by 2?

_____

_____

d. Use your calculator to complete the table below.

	2^{nth}	Square Root		3^{nth}	Square Root		5^{nth}	Square Root
d	$2^1 =$	$\sqrt{d} =$		$3^1 =$	$\sqrt{d} =$		$5^1 =$	$\sqrt{d} =$
e	$2^{1/2} =$	$\sqrt{e} =$		$3^{1/2} =$	$\sqrt{e} =$		$5^{1/2} =$	$\sqrt{e} =$

e. What does the two in the denominator of the exponent mean? How does it affect the number?

_____

_____

Name _____

Date _____

Fractional Exponents *(cont.)*

Directions: Compute each of the following numbers on the graphing calculator to test your theory on the effect of dividing the exponent by two. To enter the fractional exponents, enter the base and then the fraction in parentheses.

f. $49^{\frac{1}{2}}$ = _____

g. $121^{\frac{1}{2}}$ = _____

h. $\sqrt{98}$ = _____

i. $98^{\frac{1}{2}}$ = _____

j. $\sqrt{7^3}$ = _____

k. $7^{\frac{3}{2}}$ = _____

Directions: Answer the following questions to draw some conclusions about fractional exponents.

l. In problem **k**, what does the 3 mean? the 2? Test your hypothesis on the graphing calculator. What did you discover?

_____

_____

m. How could you write $\sqrt[5]{2^6}$ using fractional exponents? How about $(\sqrt[5]{2})^6$? Should these have the same value? Why or why not? Check the values on your graphing calculator.

_____

_____

n. In the expression $27^{\frac{5}{3}}$, what does the 5 represent? What does the 3 represent? Find at least three ways to evaluate this expression, where at least one of them does NOT require the use of the calculator. Record the ways below.

_____

_____

_____

_____

Name _____

Date _____

Math Carnival

Directions: Solve the problems below. Show your work.

   a. You are running a booth at a school carnival where paint balls are thrown at a target. You have been allotted 20 gallons of paint and you would like to prepare 150 spherical balloons. To fill the balloons, you need to know the diameter of the filled balloon. Remember that the formula for the volume of a sphere is $V = \frac{4}{3}\pi r^3$ and that there are 231 cubic inches in a gallon. What should you choose for the diameter of your balloons?

   b. The centerpiece of the carnival will be a big cement sphere that you will paint red. You wish to have the largest possible sphere, but you only have one gallon of red paint. The paint can says that one gallon of paint will cover 450 square feet of cement. The formula for the surface area of a sphere is $A = 4\pi r^2$. What is the radius of the largest possible sphere?

   c. You must also build a box for the ticket taker to put the ticket stubs in. It needs to be a cube. You plan to put a top on the box and then cut a slit for the tickets. You have 45 square feet of plywood. What are the dimensions of the largest possible box? What is the volume of the box?

   d. Another option for the box in problem **c** is to make it a cube with no restrictions on the height. If you are able to use all the plywood, what would the dimensions of the cube be? What would the volume of the box be?

   e. In another carnival game, a water balloon is going to be released from a platform that is 40 feet tall, and the contestant will throw a dart to try to hit it on the way down. If you will release the dart from your eye level of 5.5 ft, how long will it take the balloon to reach your release height? The distance that a falling object has traveled is found by the formula $d = 16t^2$, where d is the distance in feet and t is the time in seconds.

Completing the Square

Unit 4

Lesson Description

- Students will solve and graph quadratic equations by factoring, completing the square, or using the quadratic formula. Students will apply these techniques in solving word problems.

- Students will graph quadratic functions and know that their roots are the *x*-intercepts.

Materials

- *Complete the Square* (pages 167–168; unt4.167.pdf)

- *Be There or Be Square!* (page 169; unt4.169.pdf)

- TI-83/84 Plus Family Graphing Calculator or TI-73 Explorer™

Explaining the Concept/Using the Calculator

Part I—Creating a Graph of a Parabola

Step 1

Ask students the following questions.

- What is a parabola? *Answer: The graph of a quadratic function*

- What is a vertex? *Answer: It is the maximum or minimum value of the parabola.*

- What type of equation creates a parabola? *Answer: $ax^2 + bx + d$*

Step 2

Model how to graph a parabola on the calculator.

- Pass out the *Complete the Square* activity sheet (pages 167–168).

- Check the **MODE** and **FORMAT** (**2ND**, **ZOOM**) to ensure all default settings (left-hand side) are set.

- Press **Y=** and clear any equations entered. Input *$x^2 - 6x + 5$* into **Y₁**.

- Press **ZOOM** and then select **6: ZStandard**.

- Have the students sketch the graph on the *Complete the Square* activity sheet.

Step 2

Step 2 *(cont.)*

Step 2 *(cont.)*

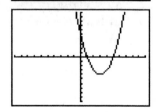

Completing the Square *(cont.)*

Unit 4

Explaining the Concept/Understanding the Concept *(cont.)*

Part II:—Finding the Vertex

Step 3   Model how to use the Calc feature to find the vertex.

- Explain that the minimum point or maximum point on the parabola is called the *vertex*. Have the students circle the vertex on their sketches.

- Access **CALC** by choosing [2ND] and then [TRACE].

- Ask the students which of the menu items might represent the lowest point. Tell the students to select **3: minimum**.

- For the prompt **"Left Bound?"**, move the cursor left of the vertex and then press [ENTER].

- For the prompt **"Right Bound?"**, move the cursor right of the vertex and press [ENTER].

- For the prompt **"Guess?"**, move the cursor to a point near the vertex and press [ENTER].

- Explain that the method the calculator uses to estimate the minimum is not exact and they should round the minimum to $(3, -4)$.

- For problem **a** on the *Complete the Square* activity sheet (page 167), mark the vertex on the graph and write the coordinates on the line below.

Step 4   Have students find the vertices of the other parabolas for problems **b–d** on the *Completing the Square* activity sheet.

Part III:—Identifying the Coefficients

Step 5   Show students how to identify the coefficients of quadratic equations.

- Tell the students that every quadratic equation can be written in the form $y = ax^2 + bx + c$.

Step 3

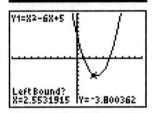

Step 3 *(cont.)*

Step 3 *(cont.)*

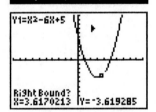

Step 3 *(cont.)*

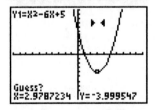

Step 3 *(cont.)*

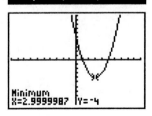

Completing the Square *(cont.)*

Unit 4

Explaining the Concept/Understanding the Concept *(cont.)*

Part III:—Identifying the Coefficients *(cont.)*

Step 6
Have the students identify the values of a, b, and c for the equations for problems **e–h** on the activity sheet, *Complete the Square* (page 168) and write them in the table.

- Then, complete the next two columns by inputting the values for a, b, and c into the equations.

- Ask the students to find the relationship between these numbers and the vertices of the parabola.

  Answer: $-\dfrac{b}{2a}$ *identifies the line of symmetry for the* vertex.

  $\left(\dfrac{b}{2a}\right)^2$ *identifies the y-intercept.*

Part IV:—Solving Quadratic Equations Graphically

Step 7
Model how to solve the quadratic equation $x^2 - 6x + 5 = 0$ graphically on the calculator.

- Press ■. Enter $x^2 - 6x + 5$ into Y_1.

- Press ■ and then (6) to graph the equation in **ZStandard** window.

- Refer to **Step 3** for these screenshots.

Step 8
Show students how to find the x-intercept on the left side of the graph.

- Access the **CALC** by pressing ■ and ■. Choose **2: zero**.

- For the "**Left Bound?**" prompt, move the cursor to the left of the zero and then press ■.

- For the "**Right Bound**" prompt, move the cursor to the right of the zero and then press ■.

- The arrows at the top of the screen show the chosen interval. There should be only one x-intercept between the right and left bounds.

- For the "**Guess?**" prompt, move the cursor close to the x-intercept on the left-side of the graph. Press ■.

Step 8

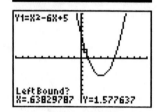

Step 8 *(cont.)*

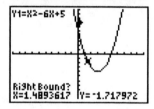

Step 8 *(cont.)*

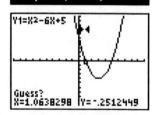

Step 8 *(cont.)*

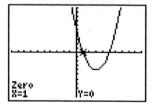

Step 8 *(cont.)*

Completing the Square

Unit 4

Step 9

Explaining the Concept/Understanding the Concept *(cont.)*

Explain to students that the x-value is a zero of the equation, $y = x^2 - 6x + 5$. It is also the x-intercept of the graph of $y = x^2 - 6x + 5$, and a solution to the equation.

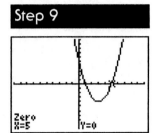

- Have the students find the other solution, by identifying the zero on the right-side of the parabola. Repeat the keystrokes in **Step 8**.

Applying the Concept

Step 1

Model how to complete the last column of the table on the activity sheet *Complete the Square* (page 168) by inputting the values for *h, k,* and *a,* into the equation, $y = a(x - h)^2 + k$.

- Explain that the equation in the last column is referred to as "completing the square."

- Tell students that by writing a quadratic equation in the form $y = a (x - h)^2 + k$, we can tell the width of the curve of the parabola and it's vertex.

- The vertex is represented by the ordered pair *(h, k)*.

Step 2

Model how to complete the square to find the solution of a quadratic equation.

- Students will record their answers in the last column of the table on the *Completing the Square* activity sheet.

- Using problem **e**, replace $x^2 - 6x + 5$ with the right side of the equation in the last column of the table on *Completing the Square*, yielding the equation $(x - 3)^2 - 4 = 0$.

- Add 4 to both sides of the equation to simplify the expression into a squared binomial. Then, take the square root of both sides of the equation. Explain the importance of using the ± symbol.

$$(x - 3)^2 - 4 = 0$$
$$(x - 3)^2 = 4$$
$$(x - 3) = \pm\, 2$$
$$x - 3 = 2 \quad or \quad x - 3 = -2$$
$$x = 5 \quad or \quad x = 1$$

Completing the Square *(cont.)*

Unit 4

Step 3

Applying the Concept *(cont.)*

Using problem **f** on *Complete the Square* (page 169), have students work with partners to complete the square and find the solution of $x^2 + 8x + 12 = 0$.

- Have the students replace the left side of the equation with the expression on the last column on the organizer and subtract 12 from each side.

- Show students how to take the square root of each side and solve for x.

$$x^2 + 8x + 12 = 0$$
$$(x^2 + 8x + 16) + 12 - 16 = 0$$
$$(x + 4)^2 + 12 - 16 = 0$$
$$(x + 4)^2 - 4 = 0$$
$$(x + 4)^2 = 4$$
$$x + 4 = \pm 2$$
$$x = -4 + 2 \text{ or } x = -4 - 2$$
$$x = -2 \text{ or } x = -6$$

Step 4

Using problem **g** on *Complete the Square*, have students work with partners to complete the square and find the solution of $2x^2 - 8x + 6 = 0$.

- Replace the left side of the equation with the expression $2(x - 2)^2 - 2 = 0$ from the last column of the table. Then add 2 to each side.

- Show students how to divide each side by 2 and take the square root of each side to solve for x.

$$2(x - 2)^2 - 2 = 0$$
$$\frac{2(x - 2)^2}{2} = \frac{2}{2}$$
$$(x - 2)^2 = 1$$
$$(x - 2) = \pm 1$$
$$x - 2 = 1 \quad or \quad x - 2 = -1$$
$$x = 3 \quad or \quad x = 1$$

Completing the Square *(cont.)*

Unit 4

Step 5

Applying the Concept *(cont.)*

Using problem **h**, on *Complete the Square*, have a student volunteer model how to solve the problem.

- Replace $3x^2 + 18x - 9 = 0$ with the left side of the equation in the last column of the table, yielding the equation $3(x + 3)^2 - 36 = 0$.

- Add 36 to each side of the equation and divide each side by 3.

- Show how to use the radical sign to take the square root of each side. Then, tell students to subtract 3 from each side.

$$3x^2 + 18x - 9 = 0$$

$$3(x + 3)^2 - 36 = 0$$

$$3(x + 3)^2 = 36$$

$$(x + 3)^2 = 12$$

$$x + 3 = \pm \sqrt{12}$$

$$x = -3 + \sqrt{12} \quad \text{or} \quad x = -3 - \sqrt{12}$$

- These solutions are irrational numbers, which do not have exact decimal equivalents.

Step 6

Model how to use the calculator to find decimal approximations to the solutions in the above problem.

- Press **2ND** and then **x²** to access the square root.

- Press **)** to close the parentheses under the radical.

```
Step 6
-3+√(12)
          .4641016151
-3-√(12)
         -6.464101615
■
```

Step 7

Have students work with a partner to check the solution to $3x^2 + 18x - 9 = 0$ graphically.

- Repeat **Steps 7** and **8** on page 162 to input the graph, $y = 3x^2 + 18x - 9$. Find both the left and right *x*-intercepts, using the zero feature on the Calc menu.

- Input the following values to adjust the window to view a complete graph:

  Xmin: –10, Xmax: 10, Xscl: 1, Ymin: –40, Ymax: 10, Yscl: 1, Xres: 1

- Discuss that the graphical solutions are approximations for the irrational numbers and that the calculator cannot find exact solutions for this equation.

Step 8

Applying the Concept *(cont.)*

Have students solve $-x^2 + 10x - 11 = 0$ by completing the square.

- Review the solution with the students to ensure they are able to successfully complete the activity sheet, *Be There or Be Square!* (page 169).

- Ask the students the values of a, b, and c. Be sure to point out that a is -1.

- Have the students rewrite the equation in the form $a(x - h)^2 + k = 0$.

- Help the students solve the equation by multiplying both sides of the equation by -1 and completing the square for the equation $-x^2 + 10x - 11 = 0$.

$$h = -\frac{10}{2} = 5 \qquad k = -11 - 1\left(\frac{10}{2}\right)^2 = -11 - 25 = -36$$

$$(x - 5)^2 - 36 = 0$$

$$(x - 5)^2 = 36$$

$$x + 5 = \pm 6$$

$$x = -5 + 6 \ \ or \ \ x = -5 - 6$$

$$x = 1 \ or \ x = -11$$

Step 9

Have the students complete the remaining problems on the *Be There or Be Square!* activity sheet.

Extension Ideas

- Explain that the steps to complete the square to solve a quadratic equation are equivalent to using the quadratic formula. Have the students solve the equations on the activity sheet, *Be There or Be Square!*, using the quadratic formula.

- For very advanced students, show how the process of completing the square leads to the quadratic formula.

Name _____

Date _____

Complete the Square

Directions: Graph each of the following equations and identify the vertex.

a. $y = x^2 - 6x + 5$

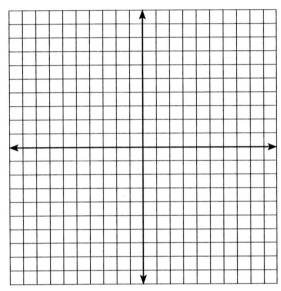

Vertex: _____

c. $y = 2x^2 - 8x + 6$

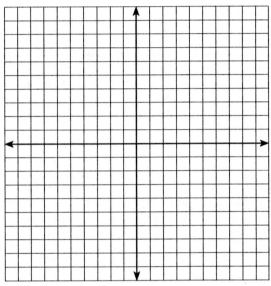

Vertex: _____

b. $y = x^2 + 8x + 12$

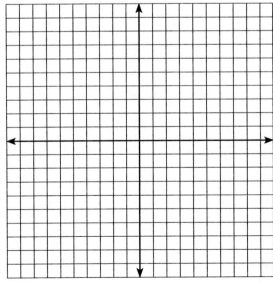

Vertex: _____

d. $y = 3x^2 + 18x - 9$

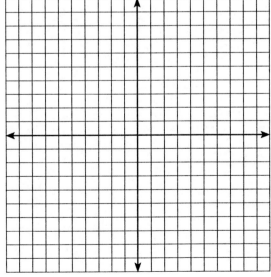

Vertex: _____

Name _____

Date _____

Complete the Square (cont.)

$y = ax^2 + bx + c$	a	b	c	$-\dfrac{b}{2a} = h$	$c - a\left(\dfrac{b}{2a}\right)^2 = k$	$y = a(x - h)^2 + k$
e. $y = x^2 - 6x + 5$						
f. $y = x^2 + 8x + 12$						
g. $y = 2x^2 - 8x + 6$						
h. $y = 3x^2 + 18x - 9$						

Be There or Be Square!

Directions: Use completing the square to find the solutions to the equations. Check your solutions graphically.

a. $x^2 + 10x - 11 = 0$

b. $-x^2 + 24x - 63 = 0$

c. $2x^2 - 6x - 20 = 0$

d. $x^2 - 6x - 7 = 0$

e. Joel is standing on a diving board 10 feet above the water level in a swimming pool. He holds a ball out over the water and tosses it straight up into the air with a velocity of 32 ft/sec and the ball hits the water when the distance is zero. The ball's height above the water is given by the formula $d = -16t^2 + 32t + 10$, where t is the number of seconds that have elapsed since Joel let go of the ball. When will the ball hit the surface of the water?

f. Anne shoots the basketball with one second left in the game. The basketball hoop is 10 feet off the ground and she shoots the ball at 5 feet. If the initial velocity of the ball is 64 ft/sec, the equation would be $10 = -16t^2 + 64t + 5$. Does Anne make the basket before the buzzer? How soon before or after the buzzer does the ball go in the basket?

Exploring Factors, Zeros, & Roots
Unit 4

Lesson Description
- Students will solve a quadratic equation by factoring.
- Students will graph quadratic functions and know that their roots are the *x*-intercepts.

Materials
- *Factors, Zeros, & Roots* (pages 176–177; unt4.176.pdf)
- *Graphs and Factors* (pages 178–179; unt4.178.pdf)
- *Factoring & Solving Quadratic Equations* (pages 180–182; unt4.180.pdf)
- *R & S* (page 183; unt4.183.pdf)
- TI-83/84 Plus Family Graphing Calculator or TI-73 Explorer™

Explaining the Concept

Step 1

Give the students the *Factors, Zeros, & Roots* activity sheet (pages 176–177). Then, explain the Factors of Zero Property.
- Write [$ab = 0$] on the overhead or board.
- Ask students if they can be sure what *a* equals, or if they can be sure what *b* equals. Discuss how they can be sure that at least one of the factors is zero.
- Explain that we can guarantee a solution by setting each factor equal to zero. Tell students that this is called the *Factors of Zero Property*.

Step 2

Model how to find the solutions of $(x - 4)(x - 2) = 0$.
- Ask them what they can conclude about this equation from the Factors of Zero Property. *Answer: Each factor can be set equal to zero.*
- Have the students write the solutions to the binomial equations $x - 4 = 0$ and $x - 2 = 0$ for problems **a** and **b** on the, *Factors, Zeros, & Roots* activity sheet.

Step 3

Have students complete the table on *Factors, Zeros, & Roots*.
- In the first column of the table, have students use substitution to show that 4 and 2 are solutions to the equation, $(x - 4)(x - 2) = 0$.
- In the second column of the table, have students multiply $(x - 4)(x - 2)$.
- In the third column, have students show that 4 and 2 are solutions to $x^2 - 6x + 8 = 0$ by substituting them into the equation.
- Explain to students that 2 and 4 are solutions or roots to the equivalent equations $(x - 4)(x - 2) = 0$ and $x^2 - 6x + 8 = 0$.
- Explain to students that $(x - 4)$ and $(x - 2)$ are factors of $x^2 - 6x + 8$.
- Students should complete statements **c** and **d** on *Factors, Zeros, & Roots*.

Exploring Factors, Zeroes, & Roots *(cont.)*

Unit 4

Step 4

Explaining the Concept *(cont.)*

Have students complete the table in **Part II** of the activity sheet *Factors, Zeros, & Roots* (page 176), using the given solutions.

- In the first column, write an equation with two factors whose solutions are 3 and 5.

- In the second column, multiply $(x - 3)(x - 5)$.

- In the third column, check the solutions by substitution.

- Have the students repeat these steps using -3 and -5 as solutions and then 3 and -5 as solutions.

- Help the students generalize their understanding by completing statement **e** on the activity sheet. *Answer: If* a *and* b *are solutions, then one equation would be* $(x - a)(x - b) = 0$.

Using the Calculator

Step 1

Show students how to prepare the calculator to graph equations.

- Press **MODE** and select the default settings (all left-hand settings).

- Access **FORMAT** by pressing **2ND** and then **ZOOM**. Using the same method, select the default settings with all the selections darkened on the left.

- Press **Y=**. Turn off any of the highlighted Plots at the top of the screen.

Step 2

Show students how to graph $y = (x - 4)(x - 2)$. (Problem **f** on *Factors, Zeros, & Roots*.)

- Enter $(x - 4)(x - 2)$ into Y_1. Press **x,T,θ,n** to insert x. Press **(** and **)** to insert the parentheses.

- Press **ZOOM** and then **4** to create a **ZDecimal** window.

- Have students sketch the graph for problem **f** in **Part III** on the activity sheet *Factors, Zeros, & Roots* (page 177).

Step 1

Step 1 *(cont.)*

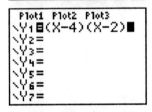

Step 2

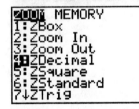

Step 2 *(cont.)*

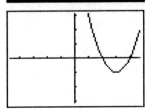

Step 2 *(cont.)*

Exploring Factors, Zeros, & Roots (cont.)

Unit 4

Using the Calculator (cont.)

Step 3

Calculate the solutions to $(x - 4)(x - 2) = 0$ by tracing to the points where the y-value is zero.

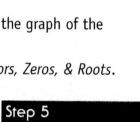

Step 3

- Press ▇TRACE▇. Move along the graph using the right and left arrows. The x-values increase by 0.1 at a time. The y-values are determined by the equations.

- Ask students to locate the points that have a y-coordinate of 0, circle them on their sketches and write the ordered pair of each point below it.

- Have students identify the solutions on the graph for problem **f** on *Factors, Zeros & Roots* (page 177).

Step 4

Using the table in **Part I** of *Factors, Zeros, and Roots*, have students find the relationship between the x-coordinate of these points and the solutions to the equation $(x - 4)(x - 2) = 0$.

- Explain that these numbers are the roots to the above equation. These numbers are also called the zeros of $y = (x - 4)(x - 2)$ because they cause the value of the equation to be zero.

- Finally, these same numbers are also the x-intercepts of the graph of the equation above.

- Have the students complete the statements **g–i** on *Factors, Zeros, & Roots*.

Step 5

Model how to graph the quadratic trinomial $y = x^2 - 6x + 8$. (Problem **j** on the *Factors, Zeros, and Roots*.)

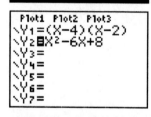

Step 5

- Turn off the equation in Y_1 by pressing ▇Y=▇, using the left arrow to move the cursor onto the equal sign and pressing ▇ENTER▇.

- Enter $x^2 - 6x + 8$ into Y_2. To enter x^2, press ▇X,T,θ,n▇ and then ▇x^2▇.

- Press ▇ZOOM▇, ▇ 4 ▇ to create a **ZDecimal**.

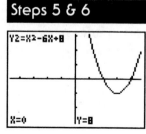

Steps 5 & 6

- Instruct the students to sketch the graph for problem **j** on *Factors, Zeros, & Roots*.

Step 6

Have students solve $x^2 - 6x + 8 = 0$.

- Use trace to find the x-intercepts.

- On their graphs on, *Factors, Zeros, & Roots*, students should circle these points and write the ordered pairs below them. Then have the class complete statement **k**.

Exploring Factors, Zeros, & Roots *(cont.)*

Unit 4

Using the Calculator *(cont.)*

Step 7

Illustrate the relationship between factors and zeros.

- Turn Y_1 back on by highlighting the equal sign and pressing **ENTER**.

- Press **GRAPH** and ask the students why they see only one graph.

- Show the students that pressing the up or down arrow while tracing switches the equation from Y_1 to Y_2 or vice versa.

- Ask the students why the ordered pairs are the same on the two graphs. *Answer: The equations are equivalent.*

Step 8

Attempt to find the *x*-intercepts of $y = x^2 - 4x - 12$ by tracing. (Problem **l** on *Factors, Zeros, & Roots*.)

- Clear any previous equations from the Y= menu and enter $x^2 - 4x - 12$ into Y_1.

- Press **ZOOM** and then (**4**) to create a **ZDecimal** window and view the graph of the equation.

- Have the students discuss why this is not a "complete" graph.

- Suggest changing the window by selecting **ZOOM** and then **6: ZStandard**.

- Ask students whether they would consider this a complete graph and whether it is adequate to find the solutions to the equation.

- Have the students attempt to find the *x*-intercepts by tracing. They will find that it is not possible in this window.

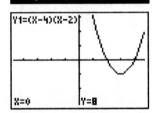

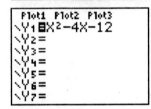

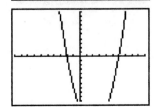

Exploring Factors, Zeros, & Roots *(cont.)*

Unit 4

Using the Calculator *(cont.)*

Step 9

Have students use the **CALC** menu to find the *x*-intercepts.

- Access **CALC** by pressing [2ND] and then [TRACE]. Choose **2: zero**.

- Tell the students to find the *x*-intercept on the left.

- When the "**Left Bound**" prompt appears, move the cursor left of the zero and then press [ENTER].

- When the "**Right Bound**" prompt appears, move the cursor to the right of the zero and then press [ENTER].

- The arrows at the top of the screen show the chosen interval. There should be only one *x*-intercept between the right and left bounds.

- When the "**Guess?**" prompt appears, move the cursor close to the *x*-intercept and then press [ENTER].

- Repeat the procedure to find the *x*-intercept on the right.

Step 10

For problem **l** on the *Factors, Zeros, & Roots* activity sheet (page 177), have students sketch the graph of the equation $x^2 - 4x - 12$.

- Students should circle the *x*-intercepts on the graph and write the ordered pairs of the points below it.

Step 11

Factor $x^2 - 4x - 12$ as the product of two binomial factors.

- Ask the students to recall the relationship they discovered earlier about *x*-intercepts and factors. *Answer: x-intercepts are the roots of the factors.*

- Have the class propose two binomial factors for $x^2 - 4x - 12$ and record it for problem **m** on the activity sheet.

- Have the students check the factors by multiplying and by graphing them in Y_2. Have them answer question **n** on the activity sheet.

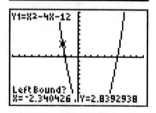

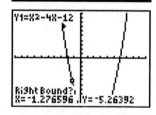

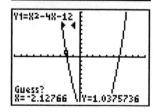

Exploring Factors, Zeros, & Roots *(cont.)*

Unit 4

Applying the Concept

Step 1 Working in small groups, have students use graphs to factor $x^2 - 8x + 12$, $x^2 - x - 12$, and $x^2 - 11x - 12$.
- Have students present their graphs to the class.

Step 2 Have students complete *Graphs and Factors* (page 178–179).
- Have students share their answers with a partner when they are finished.
- Discuss students' statements as a whole group.

Step 3 Show the students how to extend factoring techniques to quadratics in the form $ax^2 + bx + c = 0$ where $a \neq 1$.
- Have students complete **Part I** of the activity sheet *Factoring & Solving Quadratic Equations* (pages 180–182).

Step 4 Show the students how identifying r and s enables them to factor a quadratic equation.
- Look at expression **a** on *Factoring & Solving Quadratic Equations*.
- Explain that the r and s for this expression must satisfy the two equations $r + s = -1$ and $(r)(s) = -6$. The only numbers that work are -3 and 2.
- Demonstrate that working backwards with -3 and 2 is another way to factor the expression.

Step 5 Have students complete **Part II** on the activity sheet *Factoring & Solving Quadratic Equations*. Help them identify the correct numbers for r and s.
- Show the students the example $6x^2 - 13x - 30$. Help them look at possibilities for r and s and identify the correct values.

Step 6 Have the students complete **Part III** of *Factoring & Solving Quadratic Equations*.

Extension Ideas
- Help students model factoring where $a \neq 1$, using algebra tiles.
- Have more advanced students begin with fractional roots and find the corresponding quadratic equations.

Name _____

Date _____

Factors, Zeros, & Roots

Part I: Solve the equations below. Then complete the table by substituting and multiplying the solutions. Finally, complete statements **c** and **d**.

a. $x - 4 = 0$

$x =$ _____

b. $x - 2 = 0$

$x =$ _____

Solutions	Substitution	Multiply	Substitution
$x =$	$(x - 4)(x - 2) = 0$	$(x - 4)(x - 2)$	$x^2 - 6x + 8 = 0$
$x = 4$			
$x = 2$			

c. 4 and 2 are _____ or _____ of $(x - 4)(x - 2) = 0$ and $x^2 - 6x + 8 = 0$.

d. $(x - 4)$ and $(x - 2)$ are _____ of $x^2 - 6x + 8$.

Part II: Complete the table by writing equations for the given solutions. Then, multiply the factors and substitute the solutions.

Solutions	Factored Equation	Multiply	Substitution
$x = 3$ and 5			
$x = -3$ and -5			
$x = 3$ and -5			

e. If a and b are solutions, then one equation would be ( )( ) = 0.

 #50024—*Graphing Calculator Strategies, Algebra*

Name _____

Date _____

Factors, Zeros, & Roots *(cont.)*

Part III: Complete the statements below and graph the equations.

f. Graph the equation $y = (x - 4)(x - 2)$ on the calculator and sketch it to the right.

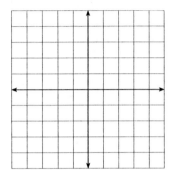

g. 4 and 2 are the _____ or _____ of the equation $(x - 4)(x - 2) = 0$

h. 4 and 2 are the _____ to the equation for $y = (x - 4)(x - 2)$.

i. 4 and 2 are the _____ to the graphs of $y = (x - 4)(x - 2)$.

j. Graph the equation $x^2 - 6x + 8 = 0$ on the calculator and sketch it to the right.

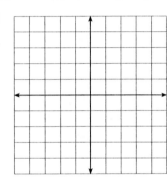

k. _____ and _____ are _____ or _____ of the equation $x^2 - 6x + 8 = 0$, zeros of _____, and x-intercepts of $y = x^2 - 6x + 8$.

l. Graph the equation $y = x^2 - 4x - 12$ on the calculator and sketch it to the right.

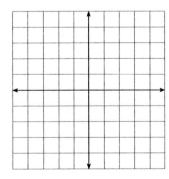

m. What are the factors of the equation $x^2 - 4x - 12$?

_____

n. Graph the factors in Y_2 of the graphing calculator. How does the graph of the factors compare to the graph of the equations? _____

Name _____

Date _____

Graphs and Factors

Directions: Factor each of the expressions by graphing them on the calculator. For each expression, give the equation that you graphed, sketch the graph, and complete the following statement.

_____ is the factored form of _____. The numbers _____ and

_____ are the zeros of _____, the x-intercepts of the graph of

_____, and the solutions to the equation, _____.

	a. $x^2 - 8x + 15$	b. $x^2 - 2x - 15$
Graphed Equation		
Graph		
Statement		

Graphs and Factors *(cont.)*

	c. $x^2 - 7x - 8$	**d.** $x^2 + 9x + 8$
Graphed Equation		
Graph		
Statement		

	e. $x^2 - 2x - 8$	**f.** $x^2 + 6x + 8$
Graphed Equation		
Graph		
Statement		

Name _____

Date _____

Factoring & Solving Quadratic Equations

Part I: In **a–g**, simplify the polynomial expressions by showing the multiplication. Use r and s to identify how the coefficient of x and the constant term are determined. Give the solution of the equation obtained by setting the equation equal to zero. Part **a** is done as an example.

Expression	r and s	Solutions to the Expression
a. $r = -3$ $s = 2$ $(x - 3)(x + 2) = x^2 + 2x - 3x - 6$ $= x^2 - x - 6$	$r + s = 2 - 3 = -1$ $(r)(s) = (-3)(2) = -6$	$x = -2$ $x = 3$
b. $(x - 1)(x + 4)$		
c. $(x + 2)(x + 4)$		
d. $(x - 3)(x - 2)$		
e. $(x - 1)(x - 6)$		
f. $(2x - 1)(x - 3)$		
g. $(4x - 3)(2x + 5)$		

 #50024—*Graphing Calculator Strategies, Algebra*

Name _____

Date _____

Factoring & Solving Quadratic Equations *(cont.)*

Part II: In the second column, find r and s and use those values in the third column to factor.

Expression	r and s	Factor
h. $x^2 - x - 6$	$r + s = -1$ $(r)(s) = -6$ $r = -3$ and $s = 2$	$x^2 - 3x + 2x - 6$ $x(x - 3) + 2(x - 3)$ $(x + 2)(x - 3)$
i. $x^2 + 3x - 4$		
j. $x^2 + 6x + 8$		
k. $x^2 - 5x + 6$		

Name _____

Date _____

Factoring & Solving Quadratic Equations *(cont.)*

Expression	r and s	Factor
l. $x^2 - 7x + 6$		
m. $2x^2 - 7x + 3$		
n. $8x^2 + 14x - 15$		

Part III: Factor and solve each of the equations using r and s. Check each solution graphically.

o. $6x^2 - 13x - 5 = 0$

p. $4x^2 - 14x + 6 = 0$

q. $4x^2 - 9 = 0$

r. $4x^2 + 12x + 9 = 0$

Name

Date

R & S

Directions: Factor each of the equations using r and s. Solve the equation and check your solution by graphing. Sketch the graph and circle the x-intercepts.

a. $4x^2 + 4x - 15 = 0$

d. $6x^2 + 13x - 28 = 0$

b. $12x^2 + 11x + 2 = 0$

e. $18x^2 - 37x + 15 = 0$

c. $11x^2 - 35x + 6 = 0$

f. $9x^2 + 14x - 8 = 0$

Determining Number of Quadratic Solutions

Unit 4

Lesson Description

- Students will use the quadratic formula and/or factoring techniques to determine whether the graph of a quadratic function will intersect the *x*-axis in zero, one, or two points.

- Students will graph quadratic functions and know that their roots are the *x*-intercepts.

Materials

- *The Canyon* (page 193; unt4.193.pdf)

- TI-83/84 Plus Family Graphing Calculator or TI-73 Explorer™

Explaining the Concept

Step 1 Remind students that in Lesson 16 (pages 160–169) and in Lesson 17 (pages 170–183), they learned three methods for solving quadratic equations: factoring, completing the square, and graphing the equation.

- Have student volunteers give a one- or two–sentence summary describing each of these methods.

Step 2 Have students work in small groups to solve the equation $x^2 - 10x + 24 = 0$ by factoring.

- Have a group present the strategy to the class. This strategy was introduced in Lesson 17, *Exploring Factors, Zeros, & Roots*.

$$x^2 - 10x + 24 = 0$$
$$(r)(s) = 24$$
$$r + s = -10$$
$$r = -6, s = -4$$
$$x^2 - 6x - 4x + 24 = 0$$
$$x(x - 6) - 4(x - 6) = 0$$
$$(x - 4)(x - 6) = 0$$
$$x = 4 \text{ or } x = 6$$

Determining Number of
Quadratic Solutions *(cont.)*

Unit 4

Step 3

Explaining the Concept *(cont.)*

Have students work in small groups to solve the equation $x^2 - 10x + 24 = 0$ by completing the square.

- Have a group present the strategy to the class.

- This strategy was introduced in Lesson 16, *Completing the Square* (pages 160–169).

$$x^2 - 10x + 24 = 0$$

$$a = 1, \ b = -10, \ c = 24$$

$$-\frac{b}{2a} = \frac{10}{2} = 5$$

$$c - a\left(\frac{b}{2a}\right)^2 = 24 - 1\left(\frac{-10}{2a}\right)^2$$

$$= 24 - 25 = -1$$

$$(x - 5)^2 - 1 = 0$$

$$(x - 5)^2 = 1$$

$$(x - 5) = \pm 1$$

$$x = 6 \ \text{or} \ x = 4$$

Step 4

Have groups work in small groups to solve the equation $x^2 - 10x + 24 = 0$ graphically.

- This strategy was presented in both Lessons 16 and 17.

- Ensure that the default (left-hand settings) have been selected for **MODE** and **FORMAT** (**2ND**, **ZOOM**).

- Press **Y=**. Input $Y_1 = x^2 - 10x + 24$. Press **ZOOM** and then choose **6: ZStandard** to view the graph.

- Access **CALC** by pressing **2ND** and then **TRACE** and then choose **2:zero** for a quadratic equation.

- Select the **left** and **right bound** values, as well as **guess** to determine the *x*-intercepts.

Step 4

```
Plot1 Plot2 Plot3
\Y1▘X²-10X+24█
\Y2=
\Y3=
\Y4=
\Y5=
\Y6=
\Y7=
```

Step 4 *(cont.)*

```
ZOOM MEMORY
1:ZBox
2:Zoom In
3:Zoom Out
4:ZDecimal
5:ZSquare
6▘ZStandard
7↓ZTrig
```

Step 4 *(cont.)*

```
CALCULATE
1:value
2▘zero
3:minimum
4:maximum
5:intersect
6:dy/dx
7:∫f(x)dx
```

Step 4 *(cont.)*

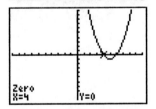

Step 4 *(cont.)*

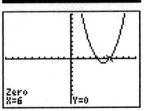

Determining Number of Quadratic Solutions *(cont.)*

Unit 4

Explaining the Concept *(cont.)*

Step 5 Discuss how each of these methods indicate that there are two solutions to this equation.

Step 6 Show the students the quadratic formula $x = \dfrac{-b \pm \sqrt{b^2 - 4ac}}{2a}$ where the a, b, and c are the coefficients from the standard form of the quadratic equation that they used in completing the square.

- Model how to use the quadratic formula to solve $x^2 - 10x + 24 = 0$.

$$x^2 - 10x + 24 = 0$$
$$x = \frac{10 \pm \sqrt{100 - 96}}{2}$$
$$= \frac{10 \pm 2}{2}$$
$$x = \frac{12}{2} \ \text{ or } \ x = \frac{8}{2}$$
$$x = 6 \ \text{ or } \ x = 4$$

- Discuss how this method indicates that there are two solutions to the equation.

Step 7 Have students work in small groups to solve $6x^2 - 10x + 4 = 0$ using the quadratic formula.

$$6x^2 - 10x + 4 = 0$$
$$x = \frac{10 \pm \sqrt{100 - 96}}{12}$$
$$= \frac{10 \pm 2}{12}$$
$$x = \frac{12}{12} \ \text{ or } \ x = \frac{8}{12}$$
$$x = 1 \ \text{ or } \ x = \frac{2}{3}$$

Determining Number of Quadratic Solutions *(cont.)*

Unit 4

Step 8

Explaining the Concept *(cont.)*

Have students work independently to solve $x^2 + 5x - 5 = 0$ using the quadratic formula.

$$x^2 + 5x - 5 = 0$$

$$x = \frac{-5 \pm \sqrt{25 + 20}}{2}$$

$$x = \frac{-5 \pm \sqrt{45^2}}{2}$$

$$x = \frac{-5 + 3\sqrt{5}}{2} \quad or \quad x = \frac{-5 - 3\sqrt{5}}{2}$$

- Remind students that these are irrational numbers and do not have exact decimal equivalents.

Step 1

Using the Calculator

Model how to solve quadratic equations with the quadratic formula using the graphing calculator.

- Solve $x^2 - 10x + 24 = 0$.
- Have students identify the values for a, b, and c in the equation.
- Have students write out the quadratic equation with the given values on scratch paper.

$$a = 1 \quad b = -10 \quad c = 24$$

$$x = \frac{10 \pm \sqrt{-10^2 - 4 \cdot 1 \cdot 24}}{2 \cdot 1}$$

Step 2

Explain how to enter the keystrokes for the quadratic equation.

- Explain that it is necessary to put parentheses around the entire numerator and also around the argument of the radical.
- Tell students that the calculator can only do one operation at a time and they should begin with the plus from the plus or minus the square root.

Determining Number of Quadratic Solutions *(cont.)*

Unit 4

Using the Calculator *(cont.)*

Step 3

Model how to enter the key strokes for the quadratic equation.

- To enter $-b$ or **10**, press [( ] to place parentheses around the numerator, and then [1], [0]. Then, press [+] to add the square root or press [−] to subtract the square root.

- To enter $\sqrt{b^2 - 4ac}$, press [2ND], [x^2] to enter the square root. Press [( ] to place parentheses around b^2 and the values in the square root.

- Enter **–10**, press [ )] to close the parentheses around b^2. Then press [x^2] to insert the square symbol.

- Input **–4 • 1 • 24** by pressing [(-)], [4], [×], [1], [×], [2], [4].

- Press [ )] twice to insert closing parentheses around the values in the square root and the numerator.

- Insert the denominator $2a$ by pressing [÷] and then [( ], [2], [×], [1], [ )].

Step 4

After finding the first solution, have students find the second solution.

- Recall the last entry by pressing [2ND] and [ENTER], and then using the arrows to move to the plus. Change the plus to a minus.

- Press [ENTER] to execute the operation.

Step 5

Have the students work in small groups to find the solutions to $6x^2 - 10x + 4 = 0$, using the quadratic formula on the calculator.

- Change the first solution to a fraction by pressing [MATH] and then [1] to select ▸**Frac**.

- To find the second solution, recall the expression and edit the operation.

Steps 3 & 4

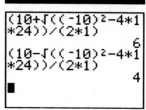

```
(10+√((-10)²-4*1
*24))/(2*1)
                    6
(10-√((-10)²-4*1
*24))/(2*1)
                    4
■
```

Step 5

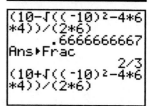

```
(10-√((-10)²-4*6
*4))/(2*6)
          .6666666667
Ans▸Frac
                  2/3
(10+√((-10)²-4*6
*4))/(2*6)
```

Step 5 *(cont.)*

```
*4))/(2*6)
          .6666666667
Ans▸Frac
                  2/3
(10+√((-10)²-4*6
*4))/(2*6)
                    1
■
```

Determining Number of
Quadratic Solutions (cont.)

Unit 4

Using the Calculator (cont.)

Step 6 Have students work in small groups to find the solutions to $x^2 + 5x - 5 = 0$ on the calculator.

- Ask the students if it is possible to have the calculator express the exact values of these zeros.

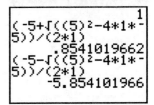

Step 7 As a whole class, solve $x^2 - 6x + 9 = 0$ graphically.

- For keystrokes on graphing a quadratic equation, review **Step 4** in the **Explaining the Concept** section.

- Ask the students what equation should be entered into **Y₁**. Have the students graph $y = x^2 - 6x + 9$ and find any x-intercepts.

- Ask the students how many x-intercepts the graph has and what that means in terms of solutions to the equation $x^2 - 6x + 9 = 0$.

- Explain that $x^2 - 6x + 9 = 0$ is a trinomial square and factors into $(x - 3)^2$ so that the equation is equivalent to $(x - 3)^2 = 0$ and has only one solution.

Step 8 Have the students use the quadratic equation to solve the equation $x^2 - 6x + 9 = 0$.

- Ask them why the two values turned out to be the same.

- Explain that the argument of the radical, $b^2 - 4ac$, is called the *discriminant*.

- Ask the students the value of the discriminant of this quadratic equation. *Answer:* $-6^2 - 4(1)(9) = 0$. *There is only one solution because $-b + 0$ is the same as $-b - 0$.*

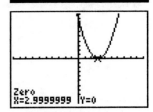

Step 9 Have the students suggest and test other trinomial squares.

- Have students graph the associated function and find the x-intercept.

- Ask the students to find the discriminant of the quadratics.

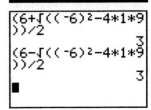

Determining Number of Quadratic Solutions *(cont.)*

Unit 4

Using the Calculator *(cont.)*

Step 10

Examine quadratic equations with no solution.

- Ask students to find the discriminant of $2x^2 + 3x + 9 = 0$. *Answer:* $3^2 - 4(2)(9) = -63$

- Ask them what they know about the square root of a negative number. *Answer: Taking the square root of a negative number results in an imaginary unit.*

Step 11

Ask them to predict the value of the x-intercept of $y = 2x^2 + 3x + 9$. Then, have the students test their predictions by graphing the equation.

- Ask students how they could change the window to see a more complete graph. *Possible Answer: Create a Standard window and then change the Ymin value to 0 and the Ymax value to 20.*

- Ask students what the lack of an x-intercept indicates about the solution to the equation. *Answer: Because there are no x-intercepts, there is no real solution.*

- Explain to the students that quadratics with negative discriminants have no real solutions.

Applying the Concept

Example 1

Step 1

Use the quadratic formula to find the time at which a tossed ball passes a wire.

- Show the students a graph of straight-line motion and a time-distance graph of a tossed ball passing a wire. This can be set up before class.

- On the **projected teacher calculator only,** switch to the parametric mode by pressing **MODE**, highlight **PAR**, press **ENTER**. Highlight **SIMUL** and press **ENTER**.

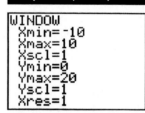

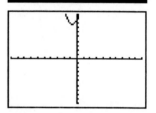

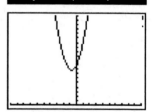

Determining Number of Quadratic Solutions *(cont.)*

Unit 4

Applying the Concept *(cont.)*

Step 2

Input the equations to create the graphs.

- Press **Y=**. By **X₁ₜ**, input **1**. By **Y₁ₜ**, input $-16t^2 + 30t - 10$. To access the *t*, press the **X,T,θ,n**.

- Use the left arrow to move the cursor to the left of X^{1T} and press **ENTER** until the symbol turns into a circle.

- By **X₂ₜ**, enter *t*. By **Y₂ₜ**, enter $-16t^2 + 30t - 10$.

- Move the cursor to the left of X₂ₜ and press **ENTER** until the symbol turns into a line with a circle. Move the cursor to the = sign and press **ENTER** to turn this equation off.

Step 3

As a whole class, view and analyze the straight-line graph of the ball.

- On the projected teacher calculator, adjust the window to the settings shown in the screen shot **GRAPH**. Scroll down and enter Ymax = 5 and Yscl = 1.

- Press **GRAPH** on the projected teacher calculator. The "ball" will rise and fall.

- Describe the graph as a ball that is being thrown upwards from 10 ft below a wire with an initial velocity of 30 ft/sec.

- Ask students how many times the ball passes the wire.

Step 4

View the time-distance graph of the ball.

- Return to the Y= screen and turn X₂ₜ back on. Reenter any character in the first pair of equations to see the graph again.

- Then press **GRAPH**.

- Trace on the graphs to explore the relationship between the time-distance and the straight line graphs.

Step 5

Explain to the students that the time-distance equation for the distance from the wire is $y = -16t^2 + 30t - 10$.

- Have students use the quadratic formula to find when the ball crosses the wire.

- Return to the graph and trace the approximate times the ball passes the *x*-axis.

Step 2

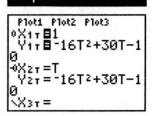

Step 3

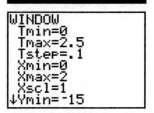

Step 3 *(cont.)*

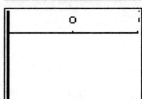

Step 3 *(cont.)*

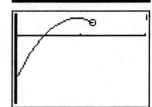

Step 4 & 5

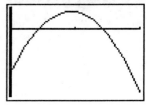

Determining Number of Quadratic Solutions (cont.)

Unit 4

Applying the Concept (cont.)

Example 2

Step 6

Create a graph of a tossed ball for students. Have students use the quadratic formula to find the time at which a tossed ball reaches a wire.

- Press **Y=** and enter the equations as shown in the screen shot to the right.

- Press **WINDOW** and change the values to those as shown in the screen shot to the right with **Ymax = 5**.

- Graph both pairs of equations and ask the students how many times the ball passes the wire.

Step 7

Have the students solve the equation $-16t^2 + 25.3t - 10 = 0$ using the quadratic formula.

- Then, trace the graph to find the time at which the ball crosses the wire.

Example 3

Step 8

Have students use the quadratic formula to show why a ball does not reach a wire.

- Input the equations and window as shown in the screen shot to the right.

- Graph both pairs of equations and ask students if the ball reaches the wire.

- Have the students show why the ball does not reach the wire by attempting to solve $-16t^2 + 20t - 10 = 0$, using the quadratic formula.

Step 9

Have students complete the *The Canyon* activity sheet (page 193).

Extension Idea

- Help students memorize the quadratic *formula* by singing the equation to the tune of *Pop Goes the Weasel*.

> *x equals opposite b plus or minus the square root of b squared minus four a c all over 2a.*

Step 6

```
Plot1 Plot2 Plot3
\X₁ᴛ■.8
 Y₁ᴛ■-16T²+25.3T
-10
\X₂ᴛ■T
 Y₂ᴛ■-16T²+25.3T
-10
\X₃ᴛ=
```

Step 6 *(cont.)*

```
WINDOW
 Tmin=0
 Tmax=1.7
 Tstep=.1
 Xmin=0
 Xmax=1.7
 Xscl=1
↓Ymin=-15
```

Step 7

```
-4*-16*-10))/(2*
-16)
          .78125
(-25.3-√((25.3)²
-4*-16*-10))/(2*
-16)
              .8
```

Step 8

```
Plot1 Plot2 Plot3
\X₁ᴛ■.6
 Y₁ᴛ■-16T²+20T-1
0
\X₂ᴛ■T
 Y₂ᴛ■-16T²+20T-1
0
\X₃ᴛ=■
```

Step 8 *(cont.)*

```
WINDOW
 Tmin=0
 Tmax=1.7
 Tstep=.1
 Xmin=0
 Xmax=1.4
 Xscl=1
↓Ymin=-15
```

The Canyon

Directions: Solve the following problem.

Judith is at the bottom of a canyon that is 50 feet deep and wants to throw a ball out of the canyon. She is not sure how fast she needs to throw the ball to get it out of the canyon. She knows that the formula for the height of the ball with reference to ground level is $d = -16t^2 + vt - 50$, where v is the velocity when the ball is released. She knows that the ball will reach exactly ground level if $-16t^2 + vt - 50 = 0$.

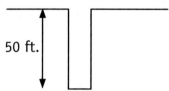

50 ft.

a. Write four equations for the height of the ball if Judith throws it upwards at 25ft/s, at 50ft/s, at 75ft/s, and at 100ft/s.

_____

_____

_____

_____

b. Graph the four equations on your calculator. Which tosses made it out of the canyon? (Hint: Set your window size to Xmin=0, Xmax=5, Xscl=1, Ymin=-50, Ymax=50, and Yscl=10)

_____

c. How fast does Judith need to throw the ball to get it out of the canyon in one second exactly? Explain how you can solve this algebraically.

_____

_____

_____

_____

Examining Exponential Growth
Unit 4

Lesson Description

- Students will learn the laws of fractional exponents, understand exponential functions, and use these functions in problems involving exponential growth and decay.

- Students will solve problems that involve discounts, markups, commissions, and profit, and compute simple and compound interest.

Materials

- Blank Paper
- *Exponential* (page 198; unt4.198.pdf)
- *Very Interesting* (page 199; unt4.199.pdf)
- TI-83/84 Plus Family Graphing Calculator or TI-73 Explorer™

Explaining the Concept/Using the Calculator

Step 1

Distribute the *Exponential* activity sheet (page 198) and blank sheets of paper.

- Have students complete the table by folding a piece of paper repeatedly and recording the resulting number of layers in the second column.

- Ask students to predict how many layers there would be if they could continue to fold the paper.

Special Note: There is an ongoing argument about the maximum number of times a piece of paper can be folded. It is generally agreed to be eight.

Step 2

Demonstrate powers of 2 on the graphing calculator.

- Have students clear the Home screen by pressing **CLEAR** twice.

- Press ⌊ 1 ⌋ and then **ENTER**.

- Recall the last answer **(ANS)** by pressing **2ND** and then ⌊ (-) ⌋.

- Press **×**, ⌊ 2 ⌋, and then **ENTER**. The results are recorded in the Answer column on the activity sheet *Exponential*.

- Press **ENTER** again and count this as the first **ENTER** on the table.

- The calculator automatically repeats the last command that recalls the CURRENT answer and multiplies it by two.

- Have students complete the Answer column.

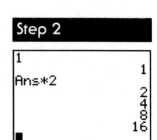

```
Step 2
1                    1
Ans*2
                     2
                     4
                     8
                    16
■
```

Explaining the Concept/ Using the Calculator *(cont.)*

Step 3

Instruct the students to continue to press **ENTER** and place the results in the Answer column on the *Exponential* activity sheet (page 198).

- Ask the students to write the answers as powers of 2, writing the expression as 2^x in the last column, **Powers of 2**, on the activity sheet.

- Point out the connection between the folds, or number of enters, and the power of 2.

- Ask the students to express the relationship as a function of *n*.

Step 4

Model how to set up the calculator to graph the exponential function $y = 2^x$.

- Press **MODE** and check **FORMAT** (**2ND**, **ZOOM**) to ensure that the default (left-hand settings) are selected.

- Before beginning the graph, press **Y=** and clear any equations highlighting the equation and pressing **CLEAR**.

- On the Y= screen, turn off all Stat plots by highlighting them and pressing **ENTER** to unselect them.

- By **Y₁**, enter 2^x. Type **2**. Press **^** for exponentiation and then **X,T,Ø,n** for *x*.

Step 5

View and analyze the graph in an appropriate window.

- Press **WINDOW**. Enter the values shown in the screen shot.

- Discuss the choices for Xmin, Xmax, Ymin, and Ymax so that the data will be visible in the window. Xscl and Yscl determine the placement of tick marks. Xres should be set at 1.

- Press **GRAPH**. Ask students why the graph is not a line or parabola.

- Explain that the equation is not a polynomial.

- Have students sketch the graph for **Part I** on *Exponential (page 198)*.

Step 4

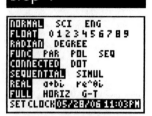

Step 4 *(cont.)*

Step 4 *(cont.)*

Step 5

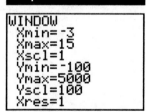

Step 5 *(cont.)*

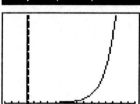

Explaining the Concept/ Using the Calculator *(cont.)*

Step 6

Compare the graph of the equation $y = 2^x$ to the first table on the *Exponential* activity sheet (page 198).

- Access **TBLSET** by pressing `2ND` and then `WINDOW`. Adjust the settings as shown in the screen shot.

- Access **TABLE** by pressing `2ND` and then `GRAPH`.

Step 7

Demonstrate how to read the table.

- Remind students that they entered the equation, $Y_1 = 2^x$, which generated the values in the table.

- Explain that on the **TBLSET** screen, 0 was the value for **TblStart**; therefore, the *x*-values begin at 0.

- Ask students how setting Δ**Tbl** at 1 affected the *x*-values. *Answer: The values are increasing by 1.*

- Use the up/down arrows to view the values in the table. Compare the numbers to the first table on the *Exponential* activity sheet.

Step 8

Show students how to use the split screen to see both the table and the graph at the same time.

- Press `MODE` and change the next to last row as shown by highlighting **G-T** and pressing `ENTER`.

- Press `GRAPH` to view a split screen with the graph on the left and the table on the right.

- Press `TRACE` and use the left/right arrows to see how the points on the graph correspond to the highlighted values in the table.

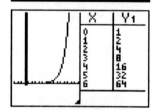

Applying the Concept

Step 1

As a whole class, investigate compound interest.

- On the Home screen, type **100** and then press `ENTER`.

- Recall **Ans** by pressing `2ND` and then `(-)`. Then, add **.06** times the answer,
  (`+`, `.`, `0`, `6`, `×`, `2ND`, `(-)`)

- Press `ENTER` to execute the command.

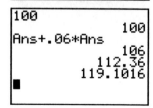

Step 2

Applying the Concept (cont.)

Explain to the students that they have found the amount they would have in a savings account offering 6% interest at the end of one year, if they invested $100. Have them enter the amount in the **Dollars** column on the **Compound Interest** table in **Part II** on *Exponential* (page 198).

- Tell students to press **ENTER** again. Explain that this is the amount they would have at the end of the second year, assuming they left all the money in the bank.

- Have students continue to press **ENTER**.

- Explain that this is an example of compound interest, compounded yearly. Discuss how it is different from simple interest.

Step 3

Have the students work in small groups to compare the table from the function $y = 100(1.06)^x$ with the **Compound Interest** table on *Exponential*.

- Students should enter the equation on the Y= screen and choose an appropriate window and graph the function.

- Ask them how the equation and the graph resemble $y = 2^x$. Have students answer the question for **Part III** on *Exponential*.

- Refer to the screen shot in **Step 1** on page 196.

Step 4

Ask the students how to adjust the compound interest equation for different investment amounts and/or interest rates.

- Have students complete the *Very Interesting* activity sheet (page 199).

Extension Ideas

As a whole class, investigate exponential growth using the spread of a rumor as a model function.

- Ask the students to propose a function that would describe one person telling a rumor to three people, with those three telling it to three more, those to three more, and so on.

- Have them enter the graph into Y_2 and compare the graph to Y_1.

- Ask the students how the graph of $y = 3^x$ compares to $y = 2^x$.

- Ask the students to predict the behavior of $y = 5^x$.

- Have the students propose situations modeled by $y = 5^x$.

Name _____

Date _____

Exponential

Directions: Follow the steps below.

Part I: Complete the table by folding a piece of paper in half repeatedly and recording the resulting number of layers. Then, enter the number of layers on the graphing calculator, multiplying each answer by two. Record the answers and then write them as powers of 2. Create a graph of the table and sketch it below.

Paper			Calculator		
Folds	**Layers**		**ENTER**	**Answer**	**Power of 2**
0	1		0	1	2^0
1			1		
2			2		
3			3		
4			4		
5			5		
6			6		
7			7		
8			8		
9			9		
10			10		
11			11		
12			12		
			x		

Part II: Complete the table and graph for compound interest, using the function $y = 100(1.06)^x$.

Compound Interest

Year	Dollars		Year	Dollars
0	100		4	
1			5	
2			6	
3			7	

Part III: How does the graph of compound interest compare to the graph of the layers of paper?

_____

_____

Name _____

Date _____

Very Interesting

Directions: Find an equation that models each of the situations below and answer the question.

a. Your very rich uncle will give you a dollar today. Tomorrow he will give you another dollar so that you have two dollars. Each successive day, he gives you enough money so that you have twice as much as the day before. Write an equation that describes how much money, y, you have on each day, x. If he begins this on February 1, 2009, how much would you have at the end of the month?

b. Suppose your uncle doubles your money weekly. Write a formula that describes how much money you would have on each day, if x stands for the number of days (not weeks) that have elapsed. How much would you have on March 29, 2009?

c. You borrow $3,000 from a cousin who is going to charge you 2.5% interest (compounded annually). You invest the money in an account that pays you 5% interest (compounded annually). At the end of five years, you withdraw your money from the account and pay back your cousin.

- What is the equation for the money you borrow?

_____

- What is the equation for the money you invest?

_____

- How much money do you have at the end of the five years?

_____

Linear Transformations

Unit 4

Lesson Description

- Students will apply transformations, that preserve distance and angles by recognizing and applying horizontal and vertical shifts, and identifying and applying reflections about the *x*-axis.

- Students will identify and predict the vertex of parabolas and absolute value graphs.

Materials

- *Transformations* (pages 206–207; unt4.206.pdf)
- *A Moving Experience* (pages 208–209; unt4.208.pdf)
- Small mirrors (optional)
- TI-83/84 Plus Family Graphing Calculator or TI-73 Explorer™

Using the Calculator/Explaining the Concept

Part I—Identifying Vertical Shifts

Step 1   Model how to enter the data into the graphing calculator.

- Press **STAT** and then **ENTER** to access the List editor.

- Clear **L1**, **L2**, and **L3** by highlighting the list name and pressing **CLEAR**.

- Enter the following data into **L1** and **L2** of the Stat List editor. Highlight the position in the appropriate column, type each number, and press **ENTER**.

$$L1 = \{-3, -2, -1, 0, 1, 2, 3\}$$

$$L2 = \{2, 2, 2, 2, 2, 2, 2\}$$

Step 2   Model how to create a connected scatter plot.

- Set up a Stat plot by pressing **2ND** and then **Y=**. Choose **1: Plot1**.

- On the **Plot1** menu, highlight the following settings and press **ENTER** to select them. Turn **On** the plot. By **Type**, select the second icon (the line graph). By **Mark**, select the first icon.

- Input **L1** (**2ND**, **1**) for **Xlist**. Input **L2** (**2ND**, **2**) for **Ylist**.

Step 1

Step 1 *(cont.)*

Step 2

Step 2 *(cont.)*

Linear Transformations *(cont.)*

Unit 4

Using the Calculator/Explaining the Concept *(cont.)*

Part I—Identifying Vertical Shifts *(cont.)*

Step 3
Set up an appropriate window to view the scatter plot.

- Press **ZOOM** and then **4** to select **ZDecimal** window.
- Press **WINDOW** and change the **YMin** to **–10** and **Ymax** to **10**.
- Press **GRAPH**. Ask the students to describe the graph.

Step 4
Have students return to the Stat List Editor and input the formula L2 + 3 into L3.

- Press **STAT** and then **ENTER** to access **Edit**.
- Position the cursor at the top of **L3** and press **ENTER**.
- Input **L2 + 3** by pressing **2ND**, **2**, **+**, **3** on the edit line and pressing **ENTER**. The calculator automatically fills the list.
- Ask the students to describe the relationship between the two lists. *Answer: Each of the values in L2 has increased by three.*

Step 5
Show the students how to set up a line graph in Plot 2.

- Set up a stat plot by pressing **2ND** and then **Y=**. Choose **2: Plot2**.
- On the Plot2 menu, highlight the following settings and press **ENTER** to select them. Turn **On** the plot. By **Type** and **Mark**, select the second icons.
- Input **L1** (**2ND**, **1**) for **Xlist**. Input **L3** (**2ND**, **3**) for **Ylist**.

Step 3

```
WINDOW
 Xmin=-4.7
 Xmax=4.7
 Xscl=1
 Ymin=-10
 Ymax=10
 Yscl=1
 Xres=1
```

Step 3 *(cont.)*

Step 4

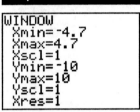

L3 =L₂+3

Step 4 *(cont.)*

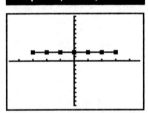

L3(1)=5

Step 5

Linear Transformations *(cont.)*

Unit 4

Using the Calculator/Explaining the Concept *(cont.)*

Part I—Identifying Vertical Shifts *(cont.)*

Step 6

Have students graph both plots and analyze them.

- Press **GRAPH** to view both scatter plots.

- Ask students, "If the first graph would have been slid onto the second, how far would it have moved?" *Answer: Three units up*

- Discuss how you could make the second graph move down six units.

- Have students test the theory by returning to the Stat List editor and changing the formula in **L3** to **L2 − 3**.

- Tell students that Plot 2 is still set up for L1 and L3 and does not need to be changed.

- Press **GRAPH**. Ask them if their graph verified their theories.

Part II—Modeling Vertical Shifts

Step 7

Create an absolute value graph of **y = | x |** to model a vertical shift.

- Enter the command **abs(x)** in Y₁. Access the absolute value command, (**abs**) by pressing **MATH** and highlighting **NUM**.

- Input **(x)** by pressing **X,T,θ,n**, **)**.

- Turn off the stat plots by moving the cursor to the top of the menu, highlighting the plots, and pressing **ENTER**.

- Press **ZOOM** and then **6** to graph the equation in a **ZStandard** window.

Step 6

Step 6 *(cont.)*

L1	L2	L3	3
-3	2	-1	
-2	2	-1	
-1	2	-1	
0	2	-1	
1	2	-1	
3	2	-1	

L3(1)= -1

Step 6 *(cont.)*

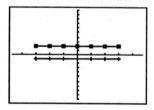

Step 7

Plot1   Plot3
\Y1◻abs(X)
\Y2=
\Y3=
\Y4=
\Y5=
\Y6=
\Y7=

Step 7 *(cont.)*

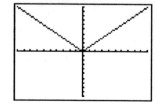

Using the Calculator/Explaining the Concept *(cont.)*

Part II—Modeling Vertical Shifts *(cont.)*

Step 8 On the projected teacher calculator ONLY, turn off the projector and enter $y = |x| + 2$ into Y_9.

- This will hide the equation from student view when you turn the projector on and return to Y= screen.

- Access **FORMAT** (**2ND**, **ZOOM**). Turn off the expressions by selecting **ExprOff**.

Step 8

Step 8 *(cont.)*

Step 9 Show the graphs to the students.

- Press **TRACE**. Toggle between the graphs by pressing the up/down arrows.

- Ask students the difference between the y-coordinates on the two graphs. *Answer: The y-coordinates on the second graph are 2 units greater than each of the y-coordinates on the first graph.*

- Discuss the equation that would produce the second graph. Then test the equation in Y_2 using the animate setting. This will show the equation in Y_2 moving along the one in Y_9 as it graphs.

- Explain to the students that the upper graph is an example of a vertical shift.

Step 9

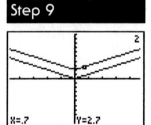

Part III—Identifying the Vertex in $y = x + c$

Step 10 Have students graph an absolute value equation in the form $y = |x| + c$ to identify the vertex.

- Tell students that every absolute value graph has a vertex, which is the point where the curve changes direction.

- Create graphs for the following equations in the same ZDecimal window.

$$Y_1 = |x| \qquad Y_2 = |x| + 1 \qquad Y_3 = |x| - 3$$

- Students should sketch the graphs for step **a** on the *Transformations* activity sheet (page 206).

Step 11 Have students identify the vertex of the equations below. They should record their answers for **Part II** on the *Transformations* activity sheet.

$$y = |x| - 10 \qquad y = |x| + 25$$

Linear Transformations *(cont.)*

Unit 4

Using the Calculator/Explaining the Concept *(cont.)*

Part IV–Identifying Horizontal Shifts and the Vertex in y = |x – b|

Step 12

Have students graph an absolute value equation in the form $y = |x - b|$.

- Create graphs for the following equations in a ZDecimal window.

$Y_1 = |x|$	$Y_2 = |x - 3|$	$Y_3 = |x + 2|$

- Students should sketch the graphs and answer the questions for **Part III** on the *Transformations* activity sheet (page 206).

- Explain that these are examples of *horizontal shifts*.

Part V—Combining horizontal and vertical shifts

Step 13

Have students identify the vertex of equations of the form $y = |x - b| + c$.

- Ask the students to predict the vertex for the following equations.

$y = |x - 7| + 2$	$y = |x + 7| - 2$	$y = |x + 7| + 2$	$y = |x - 7| - 2$

- Students should graph the equations to verify their answers. Be sure that students identify the vertical and horizontal shifts.

- Have students answer the questions for **Part IV**, question **k** on the *Transformations* activity sheet (page 207) and complete the statement about the vertex.

Part VI—Creating Reflections About the X-axis

Step 14

Ask the students to predict the graph of $y = -|x|$. Be sure to point out that the negative is outside the absolute value sign.

- Have the students graph $y = |x|$ and $y = -|x|$ in the same ZDecimal window and sketch the graph for **Part VII** on the *Transformations* activity sheet.

- Have them fold the sketch along the *x*-axis.

- Use the Trace feature to toggle between the curves.

- Ask students what effect the negative in the equation had on the graph? *Answer: It caused the graph to face downward from the x-axis.*

- Explain that these graphs are *reflections about the x-axis*, because they are mirror images of one another, if you considered the *x*-axis to be the mirror.

Using the Calculator/Explaining the Concept *(cont.)*

Part VI—Creating Reflections About the *X*-axis *(cont.)*

Step 15 Ask students to predict the graph of $y = -|x + 2| - 3$.

Have students check their predictions by graphing the equation.

Special Note: If you have mirrors, you could use them in addition to the folding.

Applying the Concept

Step 1 Have the students complete the *A Moving Experience* activity sheet (pages 208–209) to practice what they have learned and to extend the concept to parabolas.

Step 2 Have student volunteers present different parts of the activity on the projected graphing calculator.

- Discuss the differences between the graphs and transformations of the quadratic equations versus the graphs and transformations of the absolute value equations.

Extension Idea

- Have students look at other graphs using transformations by replacing the variable *x* with $|x - a|$ everywhere it appears in the equation. It is easy to look at shifts of many graphs. If looking at reflections, remember to put a negative in front of the entire right side of the equation in parentheses, and for a vertical shift, input any number.

Name _____

Date _____

Transformations

Directions: Follow the directions for each part.

I. Graph the following equations in a ZDecimal window, and sketch the graph below.

| $Y_1 = |x|$ | $Y_2 = |x| + 1$ | $Y_3 = |x| - 3$ |

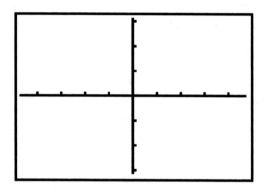

a. What is the vertex of $y = |x|$?

_____

b. What is the vertex of $y = |x| + 1$?

_____

c. What is the vertex of $y = |x| - 3$?

_____

II. Answer the following questions.

d. Where would the vertex occur on the graph of $y = |x| - 10$? _____

e. Where would the vertex occur on the graph of $y = |x| + 25$? _____

f. How can you tell if the graph will move up or down? _____

_____

III. Graph the following equations in a ZDecimal window and sketch the graph below.

| $Y_1 = |x|$ | $Y_2 = |x - 3|$ | $Y_3 = |x + 2|$ |

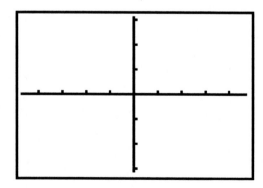

g. What is the vertex of $y = |x|$?

_____

h. What is the vertex of $y = |x - 3|$?

_____

i. What is the the vertex of $y = |x + 2|$?

_____

Transformations *(cont.)*

IV. Answer the questions below.

j. Where would the vertex occur on the graph of $y = |x - 10|$?

_____

k. Where would the vertex occur on the graph of $y = |x + 25|$?

_____

l. How can you tell if the vertex will move to the left or right?

_____

V. Identify the vertex of each equation without graphing.

$y = |x - 7| + 2$ _____ $y = |x + 7| - 2$ _____

$y = |x + 7| + 2$ _____ $y = |x - 7| - 2$ _____

VI. Complete the following statement.

In an equation of the form $y = |x - b| + c$, _____ determines the vertical shift. If the sign in front of it is a plus, it moves to the _____, and if it is a minus; it moves to the _____. _____ determines the horizontal shift. If the sign in front of it is a plus, it moves to the _____, and if it is a minus it moves to the _____.

VII. Graph the following equations in the same ZDecimal window; then sketch the graph below.

$$y = |x| \text{ and } y = -|x|$$

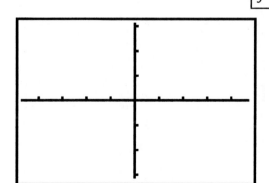

m. Fold the graph along the *x*-axis. What happens to the graphs?

_____

_____

Name _____

Date _____

A Moving Experience

Directions: Identify the vertex of each of the equations and make a sketch of the graph. Use your graphing calculator to check the graph.

a. $y = |x - 3| - 4$

Vertex: _____

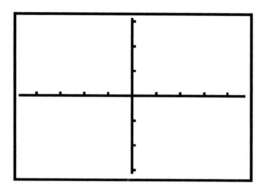

b. $y = -|x - 3| - 4$

Vertex: _____

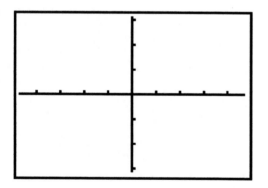

c. $y = |x + 2| + .5$

Vertex: _____

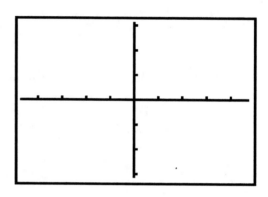

d. $y = -|x + 2| + .5$

Vertex: _____

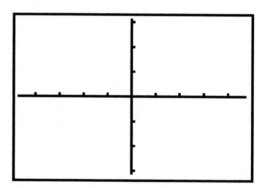

e. Graph the $y = x^2$ in a ZDecimal window. Its lowest point is its vertex. What is its ordered pair?

_____

f. On the same coordinate plane, graph $y = x^2 + 1$ and $y = x^2 - 2$. Give the vertex of each and explain the vertical shift.

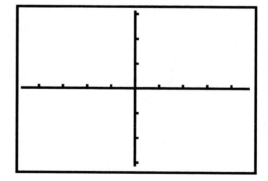

_____

Name _____

Date _____

A Moving Experience *(cont.)*

g. On the coordinate plane below, graph the following equations. Give the vertex of each and explain the horizontal shift.

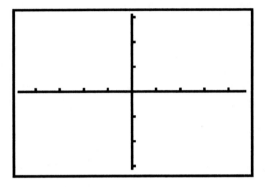

Equation	Vertex	Horizontal Shift
$y = x^2$		
$y = (x - 2)^2$		
$y = (x + 3)^2$		

h. Without using the calculator, sketch the graph of $y = -x^2$ on the coordinate plane below.

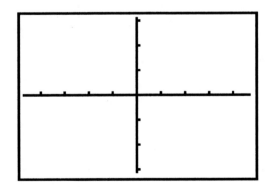

i. Predict what the graph of $y = -(x - 2)^2 + 3$ will look like and check it on your graphing calculator.

Appendices

Works Cited

Florian, J.E., and C.B. Dean. 2001. *Standards in Classroom Practice Research Synthesis: Chapter 2, Mathematics Standards in Classroom Practice*. McREL Publishing.

Marzano, R. J. 2003. *What Works in Schools: Translating Research into Action*. Alexandria, VA: Association for Supervision and Curriculum Development.

National Council of Teachers of Mathematics. 2000. *Principles and Standards for School Mathematics: Number and Operations Standard*.

National Council of Mathematics Teachers. 2003. *NCTM Position Statement: The Use of Technology in the Learning and Teaching of Mathematics*. October.

National Council of Mathematics Teachers. 2005. *NCTM Position Statement: Highly Qualified Teachers*. July.

Seely, C. 2004. *Engagement as a Tool for Equity. NCTM News Bulletin*. Reston, VA: National Council of Teachers of Mathematics. November.

Sutton, J. and A. Krueger. 2002. *EDThoughts: What We Know About Mathematics Teaching and Learning*. Aurora, CO: Mid-continent Research for Education and Learning.

Waits, B. and F. Demana. 1998. *The Role of Graphing Calculators in Mathematics Reform*. Colombus, OH: The Ohio State University. (ERIC Document Reproduction Service No. ED458108).

Waits, B. and H. Pomerantz. 1997. *The Role of Calculators in Math Education*. Colombus, OH: The Ohio State University. Prepared for the Urban Systemic Initiative/ Comprehensive partnership for Mathematics and Science Achievement (USI/CPMSA). Retrieved September 12, 2006 from *http://education.ti.com/educationportal/sites/US/nonProductSingle/ research_therole.html*

Teacher Resource CD Index

Activity Sheet Title	Filename	Activity Sheet Title	Filename
Lesson 1		**Lesson 11**	
Variables One	unt1.36.pdf	Absolutely!	unt2.121.pdf
Popcorn Varies Too!	unt1.38.pdf	Inside/Outside	unt2.122.pdf
Variables Rock	unt1.39.pdf	**Lesson 12**	
Lesson 2		In the Mix!	unt3.131.pdf
Variables Too!	unt1.44.pdf	**Lesson 13**	
Like Terms Cards	unt1.46.pdf	Mixed Shirts	unt3.138.pdf
Color It	unt1.48.pdf	**Lesson 14**	
Lesson 3		Just Nutty!	unt3.146.pdf
It's Direct!	unt1.55.pdf	A New Dimension	unt3.148.pdf
Lesson 4		**Lesson 15**	
Show Me	unt1.63.pdf	Growing Roots	unt4.155.pdf
Ups and Downs	unt1.65.pdf	Fractional Exponents	unt4.157.pdf
Lesson 5		Math Carnival	unt4.159.pdf
Check It Out!	unt1.71.pdf	**Lesson 16**	
Lesson 6		Complete the Square	unt4.167.pdf
Up, Down, & Across	unt2.79.pdf	Be There or Be Square!	unt4.169.pdf
Changes	unt2.80.pdf	**Lesson 17**	
Lesson 7		Factors, Zeros, & Roots	unt4.176.pdf
Baby Steps	unt2.86.pdf	Graphs and Factors	unt4.178.pdf
Walk This Way!	unt2.88.pdf	Factoring & Solving Quadratic Equations	unt4.180.pdf
Lesson 8			
Linear Equations	unt2.96.pdf	R & S	unt4.183.pdf
Graph It	unt2.97.pdf	**Lesson 18**	
Lesson 9		The Canyon	unt4.193.pdf
Graphing Inequalities	unt2.104.pdf	**Lesson 19**	
At The Movies	unt2.106.pdf	Exponential	unt4.198.pdf
Lesson 10		Very Interesting	unt4.199.pdf
Absolute Value	unt2.112.pdf	**Lesson 20**	
Which Way Did They Go?	unt2.114.pdf	Transformations	unt4.206.pdf
		A Moving Experience	unt4.208.pdf

Templates & Manipulatives

Large Coordinate Plane

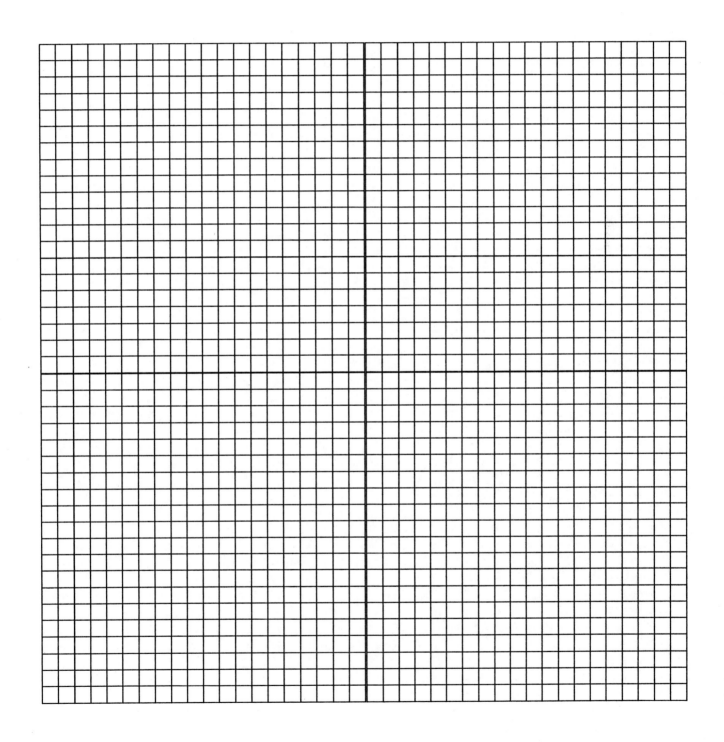

Templates & Manipulatives *(cont.)*

Small Coordinate Planes

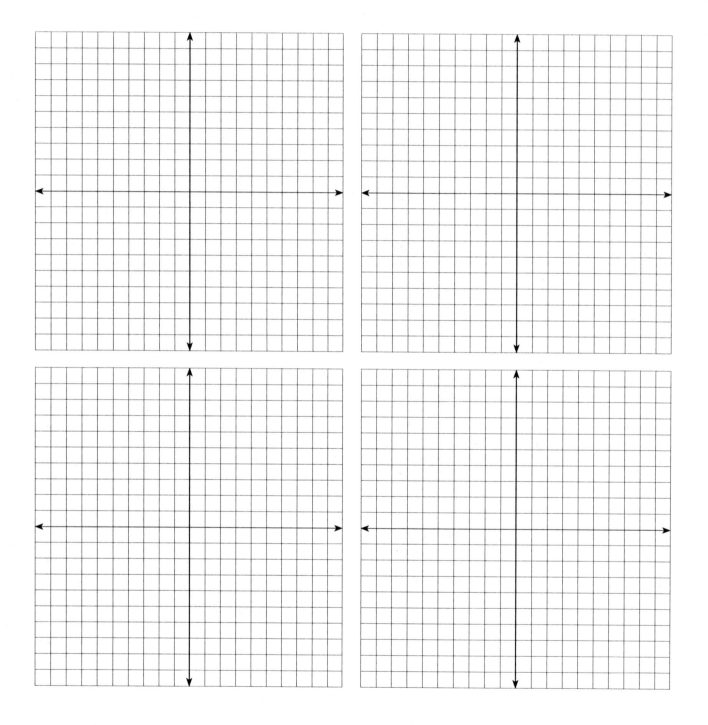

Algebra Tiles

Directions: Cut out the algebra tiles. Color one side of the large squares blue and the other side of the large squares red. Color one side of the small squares tan and the other side of the small squares red. Color one side the rectangles green and the other side of the rectangles red. The large square represents x^2. The rectangle represents x. The small square represents 1.

Using the CBR2 with Easy Data Application

Overview

The **CBR2** is a motion detector that collects data by emitting sound and calculating the distance that the sound wave traveled before it bounced back to the device. It is easy to use and provides real-world data for the study of functions.

Getting Started

1. Link the CBR2 with the TI-84 Plus and select **Easy Data** from the Applications menu. The **Easy Data** screen displays the distance from the motion detector to the nearest object. When the **CBR2** is moved, the gauge will change values.

2. Press the **SETUP** soft key at the bottom of the screen to display five choices. Press the **DIST** soft key to set the units of measure in meters or feet.

Time Graph

1. Under the **Setup** menu, **Time Graph** gives three settings, **Sample Interval**, **Number of Samples**, and **Experiment Length**. Press the **EDIT** soft key to select these individually.

2. The **Sample Interval** setting indicates the number of seconds that will elapse between readings. The **Number of Samples** setting determines how many samples will be collected. The **Experiment Length** is automatically determined by the values that are entered into the first two settings.

3. Press **OK** to return to the **Easy Data** screen. Press **START** to begin collecting and graphing the data. Time is represented on the horizontal axis and distance on the vertical axis.

4. After the graph is completed, the **PLOTS** soft key permits three different graphs to be drawn: distance vs. time, velocity vs. time, and acceleration vs. time.

5. Press the **MAIN** soft key to return to the **Easy Data** screen. Press the **GRAPH** soft key to view the Graph screen. Begin to collect new data by pressing **Start**.

Exiting the Application

- Press the **Quit** soft key and the calculator will display the lists in which the various data has been stored. Press **OK** to exit the **Easy Data** application and return to the Home screen.

Special Features

- In the **Setup** menu, the **Distance Match** feature will display a preset time-distance graph and will invite students to walk back and forth from the motion detector to try to reproduce that graph.

- The **Ball Bounce** feature collects data as a ball is bounced beneath the motion detector.

- The **Zero** feature allows the user to set another reference point as the zero value. If a wall three feet away is to be the reference point, it can be set at zero. Then, the readings would indicate how far an object is from the wall rather than from the CBR2.

- The **Help** feature, under the **File** soft key, has four screens of information about **Easy Data**.

- The **CBR** will also work with this application. Its performance will not be the same as with previous software.

The CBL/CBR Application with Temperature Probe and CBR Sensor

Overview

- CBL is an abbreviation for Calculator Based Laboratory and is a tool for mathematics and science classrooms that collects data to be sent to the calculator. The **CBL** is designed to be used with a variety of sensors, including motion, light, temperature, voltage, and many others that are listed on the Vernier website (**http://www.vernier.com**).

- CBR is an abbreviation for Calculator Based Ranger and is used in mathematics and science classrooms as well. It is a small motion detector that connects to the calculator and collects motion data. This works independently of the CBL.

- This application works only if the CBL or CBR device is connected to the calculator with a black link cord.

Getting Started

1. Insert one end of the black link cord into the Input/Output port of the CBL, which is located at the bottom of the device.

2. Insert the other end in the Input/Output port located at the top of the TI-83/84 Plus Family calculator or at the bottom of the TI-73 Explorer™.

Using the CBL with Temperature Probe

1. Select the CBL/CBR application. The title screen will appear, giving the version of the application. Press any key to continue.

2. The **CBL/CBR APP:** screen will appear, giving four options. The **GAUGE** feature gives data readings in real time, but it does not store the data. The **DATA LOGGER** feature collects data from the CBL and stores it in lists. **RANGER** collects data through the **CBR** only. **QUIT** returns the calculator to the Home screen.

3. Select the **GAUGE** feature and then highlight **Temp** to select the type of probe.

4. The following default settings will already be selected. The **Bar** setting will display the data on a bar graph. The **Min=0** and **Max=100** will only display temperature readings between 0 and 100 degrees. The **UNITS: ºC** setting will display the readings in Celsius. The **Directions On** setting will tell the calculator to give step-by-step directions.

5. To change a setting, highlight the new setting and press **ENTER** to select it. To proceed to the next screen highlight **Go** and press **ENTER**. (If the cord has not been connected, you will be instructed to do this in the course of the directions given here.)

6. Follow the directions that guide the user though the setup and connecting of the probe.

The CBL/CBR Application with Temperature Probe and CBR Sensor *(cont.)*

7. Press **ENTER** to stop the data collection temporarily, and the user can then designate a Reference # to locate this data point later. (These reference numbers are automatically stored in a list called **TREF**). Pressing **ENTER** reactivates the gauge.

8. To exit the gauge, press **ENTER**, and while the **Reference #** label is shown, press **2ND** and then **MODE (QUIT)** to return to the original menu.

9. Select the **DATA LOGGER** option. The list of default settings are similar to the **Gauge** settings. The **INTRVL** setting controls the number of seconds between readings. The **#SAMPLES** setting controls the number of data items.

10. Select **Go** and follow the step-by-step instructions. The calculator will display a line graph showing the data points with real time on the horizontal axis and temperature on the vertical axis.

11. Press **ENTER** to return to the Settings menu.

12. Choose **QUIT** to leave this application.

13. The CBL/CBR data has been saved in lists entitled **TTEMP** (time) and **TEMP** (temperature) in the Stat List editor (**2ND**, **STAT**, and then **ENTER**) on the calculator.

Using the CBR Application and Probe

1. To use the **CBR**, select **Ranger** from the original menu and then press **ENTER**. The menu will display several options. Select 1: **SETUP/SAMPLE**.

2. Each setting in the list has additional options available. To view these options, use the arrow keys to move the dark triangle cursor next to the setting and then press **ENTER**. Continue to press **ENTER** to toggle through the options.

3. The **REAL TIME** setting displays the graph as data is collected, but the time is preset at 15 seconds. If **REAL TIME** is not chosen, the graph is displayed at the end of data collection, but the time may be chosen from 1 to 99 seconds.

4. The **DISPLAY** setting gives the choice of distance, velocity, or acceleration, although data will be collected on all three. Choose DIST (distance).

5. The **BEGIN ON** setting instructs the calculator to begin data collection pressing **ENTER** on the calculator, after pressing the **TRIGGER** button on the CBR, or after a 10 second delay when the **DELAY** button is pressed.

6. The **UNITS** setting can be set to collect data in either meters or feet.

7. Use the arrows to move to **START NOW**, and then press **ENTER**. The CBR detects the distance between the **CBR** and the object toward which it is pointed.

8. This data is graphed with time as the horizontal axis and distance (if this is the selection) on the vertical axis.

The CBL/CBR Application with Temperature Probe and CBR Sensor *(cont.)*

9. Use the arrows to move right and left to trace the points that have been collected.

10. Press **ENTER** to return to a new menu. Among the choices is **REPEAT SAMPLE**, which does just that, and **MAIN MENU**, that takes the user back to the original **CBR** menu.

11. Select **QUIT** to leave the application. A note will be displayed to explain that the data has been stored in **L1**, **L2**, **L3**, and **L4**.

Special Features

- The **DISTANCE MATCH** in the **APPLICATIONS** selection on the **CBR** main menu displays a time-distance graph on the screen and challenges a student to try to match the graph by walking to and from the **CBR**.

- The **BALL BOUNCE** in the **APPLICATIONS** selection on the **CBR** main menu is used to analyze the motion of a ball bounced beneath the **CBR**.

- A part of the **BALL BOUNCE** called **SELECT DOMAIN** allows the user to select a portion of the data that is of interest by selecting left and right bounds. However, this erases the rest of the data.

Troubleshooting

Why is the calculator not detecting the device?

The most frequent problem that occurs is that the link cords have not been pushed in all the way in either the calculator or the detecting device.

What is the meaning of the message "Memory Error" that sometimes appears on my screen?

Occasionally a Memory Error occurs because the calculator does not have enough RAM to run the program. Opening Memory Management and deleting or archiving unnecessary data, pictures, programs, etc., in Memory Management usually solves this problem.

Sometimes the data does not reflect the actual distances of the object from the CBR. Why does this happen?

There may be another object (like the edge of a desk) between the CBR and the object in the experiment. The CBR will pick up the distance from itself to the nearest object. Be sure that there are no interfering objects in front of the detector. Furthermore, the CBR is accurate for objects between 1.5 and 15 feet from the detector. Outside this range, data is not reliable. The latest edition of the CBR, the CBR2, is capable of collecting accurate data at a distance closer than 1.5 feet.

Appendix D Glossary

absolute value—the distance of a number from 0 on the number line; always a positive number

algebraic expression—any term, or combination of terms, using variables that express an operation or series of operations

Ans*—2ND of the negative key (-) that serves as a variable to hold the last answer that was given on the Home screen of the calculator

APPS*—the key that opens the menu of calculator software contained in the calculator; each piece of software is also called an APP, short for application

area—the number of square units needed to cover a surface

Ask*—a setting on the Tblset screen that allows the user to control values that will be displayed in a table as it is being created

arrow keys*—sometimes called the cursor keys, these are the four keys on the upper right of the calculator that move the cursor in various calculator screens

Auto*—a setting on the Tblset screen that has the calculator automatically run a table for the conditions that have been entered

base (of an exponent)—the number, or term, that is multiplied; for example, in 5^2, the base is 5

binomial—a polynomial with the sum or difference of two terms; for example, $5x - 3$

Boolean logic—assigns a value to an algebraic statement according to whether it is true or false

Catalog*—the 2ND of the zero key. Gives an alphabetical listing of all the terms in the calculator followed by a listing of all the symbols contained in the calculator

Clear*—removal of either the last command line from the screen or the entire contents of the screen; it also refers to the button below the arrow keys

Clrdraw*—the command in the Draw menu that removes the contents from a graph screen

coefficient—a number in front of a variable; for example, in $5x^3 + 9x^2 - 7x + 1$, the coefficient of x^3 is 5, the coefficient of $x2$ is 9, and the coefficient of x is -7

collecting like terms—when working with an expression, adding or subtracting terms that have the same variable and are raised to the same power

common denominator—in fractions, a number divisible by all the denominators; for example, 12 is the least common denominator of $\frac{1}{4}$ and $\frac{1}{6}$

common factor—a number that divides evenly into all the given terms; for example, 3 is a common factor of 9 and 12

[1] The astrix (*) indicates that the definition relates to the graphing calculator.

Glossary *(cont.)*

constant—a quantity that always stays the same

contrast*—refers to the degree of lightness and darkness of the screen display; this is controlled by the 2ND and the up/down arrow keys

cube—a solid figure with six congruent square faces

cursor*—the symbol displayed on the screen that indicates where the next keystrokes will appear

decimal (decimal number)—a number with one or more digits to the right of the decimal

default*—refers to the automatic settings of the calculator

DEL (delete)*—an action that removes a single character from the calculator screen; also refers to the calculator key that brings about this action

ΔX (delta x)*—the symbol for the increment in the value of x that is used in building a table; it is found in the TblSet screen

deltaList*—command which computes the change between each successive element in the list

Depend*—found on the TblSet screen, this refers to the dependent variable of a function or the y-variable

dependent variable—a variable in a function, whose value is affected by the value of the related independent variable

diameter—the length of a line segment whose endpoints are on the circle and which contains the center

dimension of a matrix—number of rows and columns of a matrix denoted by $a \times b$ where a is the number of rows and b is the number of columns

direct variation—a linear function defined by an equation of the form $y = kx$

discriminant of quadratic equation—$b^2 - 4ac$

domain—the possible values for x in a function; the set of values for the independent variable of a given function

Draw menu*—calculator menu containing commands used to draw on the graphing screen

edit*—to write in data, particularly in a list; this is a menu choice on the Stat menu of the calculator

ENTER*—the key found on the lower right corner of the calculator, this key executes the existing command on the calculator screen, or in the case of applications, moves to a new screen or action for the application

[2] The astrix (*) indicates that the definition relates to the graphing calculator.

equality—a statement in which two quantities or mathematical expressions are equal; for example, $x - 8 = 12$ means that $x - 8$ must have the same value as 12

equation—a mathematical statement where the left side of the equal sign has the same value as the right

equivalent—equal in value; for example, $4 + 6$ is equivalent to $5 \cdot 2$

evaluate—to find the value of a mathematical expression; for example, when evaluating an analgebraic expression for a set of given values, substitute the given values and calculate the expression

exponent—the number of times a term is multiplied by itself; for example, in 3^4, the exponent is 4

factor—an integer or term that divides into another with no remainder; for example, 7 is a factor of 21

factoring—writing a polynomial expression as a product of its factors; for example, $4x^2 - 9x - 28 = (4x + 7)(x - 4)$

factors of zero property —a rule stating that if a product is 0, then at least one of its factors is zero

formula—mathematical statement, equation, or rule using variables; for example, $A = \pi r^2$ is the formula for the area of a circle

fraction—a number that identifies part of a whole or part of a group

"Friendly" window*—a window setting that yields coordinate values that are integers, or fixed decimals, when a graph is traced

function*—an expression given in the Y= screen of the calculator that represents a rule which gives y-values for given x-values

function (of x)—a relation in which every value for the variable (x) has only one value for the variable of y; for example, the total sales are a function of the number of products sold

graph—a pictorial representation of a numerical relationship among two or more terms or sets of data; a key on a graphing calculator that displays a graph screen

graph*—the key on the upper right of the calculator that displays the graph screen

graph style*—one of seven options for determining the appearance of a graphed function; the symbols are given to the left of the y-expressions on the Y= screen

grid*—found under the Format menu, this enhances the graph screen by placing coordinate points on the screen in line with the x- and y-scales that have been set

---

[3] The astrix (*) indicates that the definition relates to the graphing calculator.

Glossary (cont.)

G-T*—short for Graph-Table and found in the Mode menu gives a screen view of a graph and a table at the same time

highlighted*—the symbol or menu item that is currently selected; it is indicated by a darkened frame

Home screen*—the main screen of the calculator where calculations are displayed and various commands are carried out

HORIZ*—short for horizontal and found in the Mode menu; it splits the screen so that two different screens can be viewed simultaneously

increment—the x-value that determines the size of a step that is used in creating a table of values

Indpt*—short for independent, this refers to the x-value of a function; it is found on the TblSet screen of the calculator

inequality—a mathematical statement that uses the symbols $<$, $>$, $\leq$, $\geq$, to compare two expressions; for example, $6 > 4$ or $x \leq 9$

INS (insert)*—the 2ND of the DEL (Delete) key that creates a new space for putting a symbol into a line or expression

integers—any whole numbers, the negative of these numbers, and zero

intersecting lines—a set of lines that meet or cross

inverse operations—a pair of operations that are opposite of each other and undo each other; for example, $+$ and $-$

length—a measured distance along a line or figure from one end to the other

like terms—terms that have exactly the same variables with the same corresponding exponents; for example, $3x^2$ and $4x^2$

line—straight path extending in both directions with no endpoints

linear combination—method of solving systems of equations by eliminating variables

linear equation—a first-degree equation with two variables whose graph is a straight line

list*—a set of numerical data that has been entered into a list column, or displayed on the Home screen enclosed in brackets and separated by commas

list algebra—refers to the process of doing algebraic processes using lists of numbers rather than single numbers as elements

⁴ The astrix (*) indicates that the definition relates to the graphing calculator.

MATH*—the key that opens an extensive group of commands that are organized under four subheadings

matrix—rectangular array of numbers

Matrix menu*—contains commands for editing and operating with matrices

menu*—a listing of choices that can be selected from a particular screen

monomial—an algebraic expression with one term that is a product of constants and multiples; for example $15a^5b^2$

name a list*—the title given to a list

Negative key*—allows signed numbers to be created and is different from the subtraction key that refers to an operation

negative numbers—numbers less than zero

ordered pair—a pair of numbers that describes the location of a point on a grid, given in the following order: (horizontal coordinate, vertical coordinate) or (x, y)

order of operations—rules describing what order to use when evaluating expressions; parentheses, exponents, multiply/divide, add/subtract

origin—in a coordinate plane, the intersection of the x-axis and y-axis, which is represented by the ordered pair (0, 0)

parabola—a symmetric curve that is a pictorial representation of a quadratic function or a second-degree equation; the shape resembles the letter U and can face either up, down, left, or right

PAR (parametric) —a mode setting that allows functions in parametric form to be created and graphed

parametric equations—express the coordinates x and y in terms of a common third variable, called the parameter

paste—the action of selecting an item from the calculator and inserting it at another place

pattern—a form or model by which elements can be arranged so that what comes next can be predicted

percent—a part of a whole expressed in hundredths

plotting—placing points on a grid or a number line

---

[5] The astrix (*) indicates that the definition relates to the graphing calculator.

point—an exact location in space that has no length, width, or thickness

polynomial—an algebraic expression with two or more terms (monomials) that are added, subtracted, multiplied, or divided

positive numbers—all numbers greater than zero

power—another name for an exponent

proportion—an equation that shows two equivalent ratios

quadrants—the four regions of a coordinate plane that are divided by the intersection of the x-axis and y-axis; numbered counterclockwise from the upper right, I, II, III, IV

quadratic—involving expressions with variables raised to the second power or squared

quadratic equation—a polynomial equation with the variable in one or more terms raised to the second power, but no higher

quadratic formula—a formula used to calculate the solution of a quadratic equation

QUIT*—2ND of the MODE key, this is an action that returns from an existing screen to the Home screen. It is often used in applications to leave an active application or return to a previous screen

radical—a symbol that specifies that the root is to be taken; if there is no index, it means the square root

radius—the distance from the center to a point on the circle

range—difference between the greatest number and the least number in a set of data

ratio—a comparison of two measures or numbers by means of division

rectangle—a quadrilateral with two pairs of parallel sides and four right angles

reflection—a transformation that involves a mirror image of a figure on the opposite side of a line

right angle—an angle that measures exactly 90 degrees

root—solution to an equation

scale—a proportion between two sets of measurements

scatter plot—a graph with one point representing each item measured; two coordinates for each point represent two different attributes of the measured item

---

[6] The astrix (*) indicates that the definition relates to the graphing calculator.

scientific notation—a form of writing numbers as a product of the power of 10 and a decimal number greater than or equal to one but less than 10

simplify—combine like terms and apply properties to an expression to make calculations easier

slope—the steepness of a line from left to right

solution—any value for a variable that makes an equation or inequality true; the answer to a problem

speed—absolute value of rate of change of distance with respect to time

square—a parallelogram with four equal sides and four right angles

square root—one of the two identical factors of a given number

squared number—the product of two identical factors

Standard window*—the default window settings in which x's range from –10 to 10 with a scale of 1 and y's do the same

STAT*—the key that accesses statistical commands and allows lists to be created and modified

Stat Plot editor*—the 2ND of the Y= key that opens up settings for up to three plots of data

STO>*—the key that allows numbers and expressions to be stored in variable locations

substitution—replacing a variable with a number

system of equations—set of two or more equations that use the same variables

table*—a column listing of x-values of a function and the corresponding y-values of the function

TblSet*—a menu of settings which allow starting points and increments to be determined in the construction of a table; automatic and asking options are also given

term—each of the members of an algebraic expression that is a number, variable, product, or quotient, but not a sum or a difference; for example, $2x$, $8y^2$, 7, $9ab$

Test menu*—a calculator menu which contains the Boolean operators =, ≠, >,<, ≤, ≥

toggle*—a term describing the action of switching from one graph to another, or in turning a particular function or command on and off

TRACE*—the key next to the Graph key that allows points on a graph to be traced and coordinates to be displayed

trinomial—a polynomial with three terms; for example, $3x^2 – 4x + 3$

[7] The astrix (*) indicates that the definition relates to the graphing calculator.

variable—a letter or symbol that stands for a number

variable*—a symbolic representation of a number, list, function, or other expression

VARS—the key that accesses a catalog of all the variables contained in the calculator

velocity—rate of change of distance with respect to time; positive when distance is increasing and negative when distance is decreasing

vertex—the point at which two line segments, lines, or rays meet to form an angle

volume—the number of cubic units it takes to fill a figure

width—horizontal measurements taken at the right angles to the length

WINDOW— the key that opens the screen, which displays the minimum and maximum settings as well as the scales for the Graph screen

x-axis—the horizontal axis on a coordinate plane

x-coordinate—the first value in the ordered pair that indicates the horizontal distance from the origin on a coordinate plane

x-intercept—x-value of point where a graph crosses the x-axis

Xmax*—located in the Window screen, this indicates the upper bound of the x-values that will be displayed on the Graph screen

Xmin*—located in the Window screen, this indicates the lower bound of the x-values that will be shown on the Graph screen**Xscl***—located on the Window screen, this indicates the value of the tic marks that are being placed on the x-axis of a graph

X,T,θ,n*—the key that represents the variable x under function mode and takes on other variable meanings in parametric, polar, and sequential modes

y-axis—the vertical axis on a coordinate plane

y-coordinate—the second value in the ordered pair that indicates the vertical distance from the origin on a coordinate plane

y-intercept—y-value of point where a graph crosses the y-axis

Ymax*—located in the Window screen, this indicates the upper bound of the y-values that will be shown on the Graph screen

Y= screen*—gives a list of 10 function locations that can be used as well as a choice of Graph styles; plots can be turned on and off from this screen

[8] The astrix (*) indicates that the definition relates to the graphing calculator.

ZDecimal*—an option on the Zoom window that creates a "Friendly" window in which the coordinates are in the form of one-place decimals

zero of a function—value which yields zero when substituted into a function

ZOOM*—the key that opens the Zoom menu which contains the various options for creating automatic window settings

ZStandard*—an option on the Zoom window that creates a window in which both the *x*- and *y*-bounds are from −10 to +10, and the scale settings are one

[9] The astrix (*) indicates that the definition relates to the graphing calculator.

Answer Key

Unit 1

Pages 36–37

I.–IV. *Answers may vary.*

  V. $4a - 3r$

Page 38

a.–d. *Answers may vary.*

  e. $5b + 6.50c + 7.25r$; *answers may vary.*

Page 39

  a.

Fine	Med.	Coarse	Total
240	210	180	630
480	315	810	1605
264	1575	288	2127
0	1680	180	1860
$24f$	$21m$	$18c$	$24f + 21m + 18c$

  c. $22.50f + 18.75m + 15.25c$

  d. $24f + 21m + 18c - (22.50f + 18.75m + 15.25c)$

  e. $1.50f + 2.25m + 2.75c$

  f.   The second way because like terms were combined.

Page 44

a.–b. *Answers may vary.*

  c.   No.

d.–k. *Answers may vary.*

Page 48

	$3pqr^3$	
$2qr^2$	$6pq^2r$	$2qr^2$
	$3pqr^3$	
	$6pq^2r$	

The total surface area is $6pqr^3 + 12pq^2r + 4qr^2$

Area
2635.6176
1676.52096
750.4

Pages 55–56

  c.

15% of *n*	*n* + 15% of *n*	115% of *n*
.15L1	L1 + .15L1	1.15L1
4.50	34.50	34.50
10.50	80.50	80.50
6.75	51.75	51.75
18	138	138
1.5	11.50	11.50
9.75	74.75	74.75
$.15x$	$x + .15x$	$1.15x$

  d.

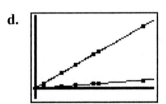

e.–f.

5.75% of *n*	*n* + 5.75% of *n*	105.75% of *n*
.0575L1	L1 + .0575L1	1.0575L1
1.73	31.73	31.73
4.03	74.03	74.03
2.59	47.59	47.59
6.90	126.90	126.90
1.5	10.58	10.58
3.74	68.74	68.74
$.0575x$	$x + .0575x$	$1.0575x$

  g.

  h. $c = 18x + 50$

  i.

  j.   The graph does not go through the origin. There is a constant term.

Pages 63–64

a. $x = -3$; $Y_1 = x + 2$; $Y_2 = -1$

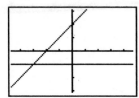

b. $x = 3$; $Y_1 = x - 5$; $Y_2 = -2$

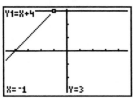

c. $x = -1$; $Y_1 = x + 4$; $Y_2 = 3$

d. $x = -1$; $Y_1 = x - 1$; $Y_2 = -2$

Page 65

a. $h + 2 = 13$, $h = 11$
b. $s + 3 = 15$, $s = 12$
c. $x + 143 = 203$, $x = 60$
d. $h + 7 = 73$, $h = 66$
e. $h + 4 = 22$, $h = 18$
f. $h - 1.5 = 9$, $h = 10.5$

Pages 71–72

a. $x = -6/11$; $Y_1 = 11x$; $Y_2 = -6$

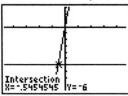

b. $x = 39/7$; $Y_1 = 7x$; $Y_2 = 39$

c. $x = 3$; $Y_1 = 4x + 5$; $Y_2 = 9x - 10$

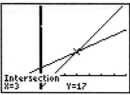

d. $x = -1.83$; $Y_1 = -9.2x - 8.56$, $Y_2 = 2.3x + 12.5$

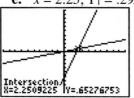

e. $x = 2.25$; $Y_1 = .29x$; $Y_2 = 3x - 6.1$

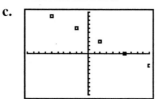

Unit 2

Page 79

a. Calculator step
b. Yes, equal increments for y and equal increments for x
c.

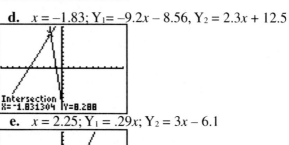

d. Falls because L1 decreases and L2 increases
e. *Answers may vary.*
f. *Answers may vary.*
g. horizontal
h. vertical
i. both lists increase or decrease; one list increases and the other decreases; all y-values are the same; all x-values are the same.

Pages 80–81

a–c. Calculator steps
d.

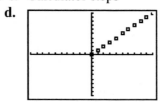

e–f.

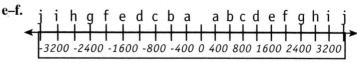

Answer Key (cont.)

Page 80–81 *(cont.)*

g. *Calculator steps*

h.

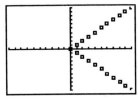

i. Slant in opposite directions; same distance from *y*-axis

j. Plot 1: rising; Plot 2: falling; because Plot 1 is increasing by 400 and the Plot 2 is decreasing by 400

k. 400 ft/min

l. –400 ft/min

Page 87

a. *x* = time elapsed (seconds); *y* = position (feet)

b. Answers may vary.

c. line rises from left to right; line falls from left to right

d. Answers may vary.

e. where line falls from left to right; the distance was decreasing

Page 88

a. The walker started 1 ft. from the end of the paper, walked away from end of it for 3 seconds and stopped at 4 ft. from the end of the paper, stood still for 3 seconds, and then walked closer to the end of the paper for 4 seconds, ending 3.5 feet from the end of the paper. Velocity: .86 ft./sec.; 0 ft./sec.; and –.125 ft./sec.

b. The walker started 4 ft. from the end of the paper, walked toward it for 3 seconds and stopped at 1 ft from the end of the paper, stood still for 3 seconds, and then walked farther from the end of the paper for 4 seconds, ending 3.5 feet from the end of the paper. Velocity: .86 ft./sec.; 0 ft./sec.; and –.125 ft./sec.

c. The walker started 4 ft from the end of the paper, toward the end of it for 3 seconds and stopped at 1 ft from the end of the paper, stood still for 5 seconds, and then walked farther from the end of the paper for 2 seconds, ending 3 feet from the end of the paper. Velocity: –1 ft./sec, 0 ft./sec., and 1 ft./sec.

d. The walker started 1 ft from the end of the paper, walked away from it for 3 seconds and stopped at 4 ft. from the end of the paper, stood still for 3 seconds, and then walked toward the end of the paper for 4 seconds, ending 1 ft. from the end of the paper. Velocity: 1 ft./sec., 0 ft./sec., and –.75 ft./sec.

Page 96

a. and c.

x	*y*	3*x* – *y*	3*x*/4 – *y*/4
–2	–10	4	1
–1	–7	4	1
0	–4	4	1
1	–1	4	1
2	2	4	1
3	5	4	1

b. They increase the same amount each time.

d. They all represent the same line.

e. slope = 3, *y*-intercept = –4; slope = –2, *y*-intercept = 3

f. *Answers may vary.*

g.

Equation	Slope	*y*-intercept
y = 4*x* – 5	4	–5
y = –3*x* + 8	–3	8
y = 5	0	5
y = 2/3*x* – 3	2/3	–3

Page 97

a. 5; –2

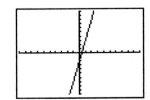

b. –1/5; –2

c. –2; 6

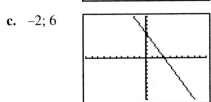

d. 4; –6

Page 97 *(cont.)*

e. 0; 8

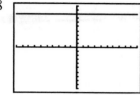

f. 0; 0

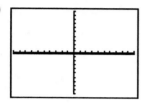

Pages 104–105

a. $h \geq 56$; Shade above 56 and right of 56 with closed dots

b. $h > 56$; Shade above 56 and right of 56 with open dots

c. $h \leq 56$; Shade below 56 and left of 56 with closed dots

d. $h < 56$; Shade below 56 and left of 56 with open dots

e. $x < 3$; Shade left of 3 with open dot

f. $x < -17$; Shade left of –17 with closed dot

g. $x > 4$; Shade right of 4 with open dot

h. $x \geq 4$; Shade right of 4 with closed dot

i. $8 > 4$; $-8 < -4$

j. $4 > 2$; $-4 < -2$

k. The right and left are the same.

l. $-4 < -2$; $4 > 2$

m. The right and left are reversed.

n. *Answers may vary.*

Page 106

Only positive numbers are possible for **a–c.**

a. $c \geq 8.75$; closed dot at 8.75. Shade right.

b. $m \leq 2$; open dot at 0, closed at 2. Shade between.

c. $35 \geq 2b + 10$; $12.5 \geq b$; open dot at 0, closed at 12.5. Shade between.

d. $-8 \leq -5t - 2$, $12 \geq t$; open dot at 12. Shade left.

Pages 112–113

a.–b. *Answers may vary.*

c.	3	**i.**	8
d.	5	**j.**	4
e.	8	**k.**	0
f.	4	**l.**	negative
g.	3	**m.**	positive
h.	5	**n.**	$x = 0, 5, 7, 3.4, 9.7, .001, 4,028$

o.

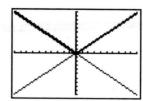

Page 114

a.

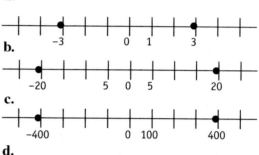

b.

c.

d.

e. $|a - 15| = 5$; $a = 10, 20$

f. $|j - 125| = 7$; $j = 118, 132$

g. $|l - .1| = 10$; $l = 10.1, 9.9$

Page 121

a. Dots at –1 and 3. 1 is halfway between.

b. Dots at –3 and 1. –1 is halfway between.

c.

Solutions are –1 and 5.

d.

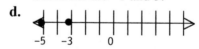

Solutions are –5 and –3.

e.

Solutions are 1 and –5.

f.

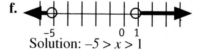

Solution: $-5 > x > 1$

g.

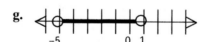

Solution: $-5 < x < 1$

Answer Key *(cont.)*

Page 122

a. $|b - 20| \leq 75$; $55 \leq b \leq 75$; She can spend between \$55 and \$95.

b. $|g - 15248| \leq 1000$; $142248 \leq g \leq 16248$; Joe must guess between \$14,248 and \$16248.

c. $|a - 8| \geq 67$; $59 \leq a \leq 75$; Band member should be between 59 and 75 inches tall.

d. $|l - .3| \leq 42$; The actual length is between 41.7 and 42.3 mm.

Page 131

a. $x + y = 31$
$4x + 6y = 138$; 24 dozen oatmeal and 7 dozen chocolate chip.

b. $p + f = 158$
$.75p + 1.25f = 138.50$; 118 plain and 40 fancy brownies.

c. $50l + 75s = 1,275$
$2l + s = 29$; 9 packages of large and 11 packs of small plates

d. $s + f = 733$
$.06s + .07f = 47.50$; 381 spoons and 352 forks.

Page 138

a. $x + y = 240$
$12x + 14y = 2964$; 198 S, M, or L and 42 XL or XXL

b. $x + y = 400$
$12x + 14y = 6000$; Solution $x = -200$ is impossible. Joe is wrong.

c. $5x = y$
$12x + 14y = 984$; 12 L and 60 XL

d. $x + 25 = y$
$12x + 14y = 2742$; 92 L and 117 XL.

Pages 146–147

a. $a + p + r = 9$; $2.45a + 1.85p + .80r = 15$; $a + p = 2r$

b. $a = 2r - p$

c.

Equation 1	Equation 2
• **Substitute for a.** $2r - p + p + r = 9$ • **Combine like terms.** $3r = 9$ • **Solve for r.** $r = 3$	• **Substitute for a.** $2.45(2r - p) + 1.85p + .80r = 15$ • **Substitute for r.** $2.45(2 \cdot 3 - p) + 1.85p + .80 \cdot 3 = 15$ • **Multiply.** $2.45(6 - p) + 1.85p + 2.40 = 15$ • **Distribute.** $14.7 - 2.45p + 1.85p + 24 = 15$ • **Combine like Terms.** $17.10 - .60p = 15$ • **Solve for p.** $p = 3.5$

d. $a + 3.5 + 3 = 9$; $a = 2.5$

e.
$$\begin{bmatrix} 1 & 1 & 1 \\ 2.45 & 1.85 & .80 \\ 1 & 1 & -2 \end{bmatrix} \quad \begin{bmatrix} 9 \\ 15 \\ 0 \end{bmatrix}$$
$$ 3 \times 3 3 \times 1$$

f. $[A]{-1}[B]$

g.
$$\begin{bmatrix} 2.5 \\ 3.5 \\ 3 \end{bmatrix}$$

You should buy 2.5 lbs of almonds, 3.5 lbs of peanuts and 3 lbs of raisins.

h. $x + y + z = 6000$
$.05x + .04y + .035z = 255$
$x = 2z$

i.
$$\begin{bmatrix} 1 & 1 & 1 \\ .05 & .04 & .035 \\ 1 & 0 & -2 \end{bmatrix} \quad \begin{bmatrix} 6000 \\ 255 \\ 0 \end{bmatrix}$$

j. $[A]^{-1}[B]$
$$\begin{bmatrix} 2000 \\ 3000 \\ 1000 \end{bmatrix}$$

Hannah's mother should put \$2,000 in First Nation, \$3,000 in the Second City and \$1,000 in Great State.

Page 148

a. $x = 1$, $y = 9$

b. $x = -3$, $y = 2$

c. $x = .5$, $y = 3$

d. $x = -5/3$, $y = -1$

e. $x = -6$, $y = -4$, $z = 7$

f. $x = 1$, $y = 5$, $z = -2$

Pages 155–156

a. $3^2 = 9$

b. $\sqrt{9} = 3$

c. The square root of 9 is 3 because 3 squared = 9.

d.–g. *Answers may vary.*

h. A possible answer may be "Numbers that cannot be written as a ratio of two integers.

i. If the number is greater than 1, the square root of the number is greater than 1.

j. $2^3 = 8$; $\sqrt[3]{8} = 2$; The cube root of 8 is 2 because 2 cubed = 8.

Page 155–156 *(cont.)*

k.–n. *Answers may vary.*

  o. 6.8556546

  p. 8.660254038

  q. 49

  r. Because 2401 is a perfect square.

Page 157

a.

	2^{nth}	$\sqrt{\ }$	3^{nth}	$\sqrt{\ }$	5^{nth}	$\sqrt{\ }$
a	256	16	6561	81	390625	625
b	16	4	81	9	625	25
c	4	2	9	3	25	5
d	2	1.41	3	1.73	5	2.24

  b. It is doubled.

  c. It was the square root of the number.

  d.

$\sqrt{2}$	1.41	$\sqrt{3}$	1.73	$\sqrt{5}$	2.24
$2^{1/2}$	1.41	$3^{1/2}$	1.73	$5^{1/2}$	2.24

  e. The 2 indicates a square root.

Page 158

  f. 7

  g. 11

  h. 9.899

  i. 9.899

  j. 18.52

  k. 18.52

  l. The 3 is an exponent. The 2 is a root.

  m. $2^{\frac{6}{5}}$

  n. 5 is the exponent and 3 is the root.

$$(27^5)^{\frac{1}{3}} \qquad (27)^{\frac{5}{3}} \qquad \left(\sqrt[3]{27}\right)^5$$

Page 159

  a. 3.89 inches

  b. 5.98 feet

  c. Each side is 2.74 feet. The volume is 20.54 cubic feet.

  d. Each side is 3 feet. The volume is 27 cubic feet.

  e. 1.47 seconds.

Pages 167–168

  a.

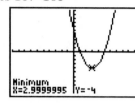

  b.

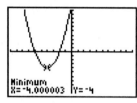

  c.

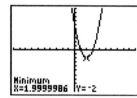

  d.

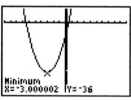

e. $y = x^2 - 6x + 5$	1	–6	5	3	–4	$y = (x - 3)^2 - 4$
f. $y = x^2 + 8x + 12$	1	8	12	–4	–4	$y = (x + 4)^2 - 4$
g. $y = 2x^2 - 8x + 6$	2	–8	6	2	–2	$y = 2(x - 2)^2 - 2$
h. $y = 3x^2 + 18x - 9$	3	18	–9	–3	–36	$y = 3(x + 3)^2 - 36$

Page 169

  a. –11, 1

  b. 21, 3

  c. –2, 5

  d. –1, 7

  e. after about 2.27 seconds

  f. Yes, after about .08 seconds.

Pages 176–177

a. 4

b. 2

Solutions	Substitution	Multiply	Substitution
$x =$	$(x-4)(x-2)=0$	$(x-4)(x-2)$	$x^2 - 6x + 8 = 0$
$x = 4$	$(4-4)(4-2)$	$0(2) = 0$	$16 - 24 + 8 = 0$
$x = 2$	$(2-4)(2-2)$	$-2(0) = 0$	$4 - 12 + 8 = 0$

c. zeros or roots

d. factors

Solutions	Factored Equation	Multiply	Substitution
$x = 3$ and 5	$(x-3)(x-5)$	$x^2 - 8x + 15$	$9 - 24 + 15 = 0$ $25 - 40 + 15 = 0$
$x = -3$ and -5	$(x+3)(x+5)$	$x^2 + 8x + 15$	$9 - 24 + 15 = 0$ $25 - 40 + 15 = 0$
$x = 3$ and -5	$(x-3)(x+5)$	$x^2 + 2x - 15$	$9 + 6 - 15 = 0$ $25 - 10 - 15 = 0$

e. $(x - a)(x - b) = 0$

f.
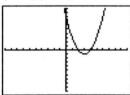

g. roots or solutions

h. zeros

i. x-intercepts

j.
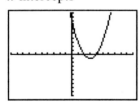

k. 4 and 2 are solutions or roots; zeros of $y = x^2 - 6x + 8$

l.
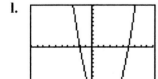

m. $(x - 6)(x + 2)$

n.
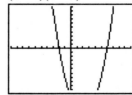
It is the same graph.

Pages 178–179

Pages 178–179	a. $x^2 - 8x + 15$	b. $x^2 - 2x - 15$
Graphed Equation	$y = x^2 - 8x + 15$	$y = x^2 - 2x - 15$
Graph		
Statement	$(x-3)(x-5)$ $x^2 - 8x + 15$ 3 and 5 $y = x^2 - 8x + 15$ $y = x^2 - 8x + 15$ $x^2 - 8x + 15 = 0$	$(x+3)(x-5)$ $x^2 - 2x - 15$ -3 and 5 $y = x^2 - 2x - 15$ $y = x^2 - 2x - 15$ $x^2 - 2x - 15 = 0$
	c. $x^2 - 7x - 8$	d. $x^2 + 9x + 8$
Graphed Equation	$y = x^2 - 7x - 8$	$y = x^2 + 9x + 8$
Graph	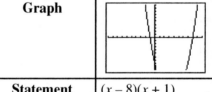	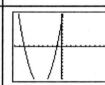
Statement	$(x-8)(x+1)$ $x^2 - 7x - 8$ 8 and -1 $y = x^2 - 7x - 8$ $y = x^2 - 7x - 8$ $x^2 - 7x - 8 = 0$	$(x+8)(x+1)$ $x^2 + 9x + 8$ -8 and -1 $y = x^2 + 9x + 8$ $y = x^2 + 9x + 8$ $x^2 + 9x + 8 = 0$
	e. $x^2 - 2x - 8$	f. $x^2 + 6x + 8$
Graphed Equation	$y = x^2 - 2x - 8$	$y = x^2 + 6x + 8$
Graph		
Statement	$(x-4)(x+2)$ $x^2 - 2x - 8$ 2 and 4 $y = x^2 - 2x - 8$ $y = x^2 - 2x - 8$ $x^2 - 2x - 8 = 0$	$(x+4)(x+2)$ $x^2 + 6x + 8$ -4 and -2 $y = x^2 + 6x + 8$ $y = x^2 + 6x + 8$ $x^2 + 6x + 8 = 0$

Answer Key *(cont.)*

Page 180–183

Expression Y	Coefficient Constant Terms	Solutions $y = 0$
a. $r = 2; s = -3$ $(x-3)(x+2) =$ $x^2 + 2x - 3x - 6 =$ $x^2 - x - 6$	$r + s =$ $2 - 3 = -1$ $(r)(s) =$ $(-3)(2) = -6$	$x = -2$ $x = 3$
b. $r = 4 \ s = -1$ $(x-1)(x+4) =$ $x^2 + 4x - x - 4 =$ $x^2 + 3x - 4$	$r + s = 3$ $(r)(s) = -4$	$x = 1$ $x = -4$
c. $r = 4; s = 2$ $(x+2)(x+4) =$ $x^2 + 4x + 2x + 8 =$ $x^2 + 6x + 8$	$r + s = 6$ $(r)(s) = 8$	$x = -2$ $x = -4$
d. $r = -2; s = -3$ $(x-3)(x-2) =$ $x^2 - 2x - 3x + 6 =$ $x^2 - 5x + 6$	$r + s = -5$ $(r)(s) = 6$	$x = 3$ $x = 2$
e. $r = -6; s = 1$ $(x-1)(x+-6) =$ $x^2 - 6x - x + 6$ $x^2 - 7x + 6$	$r + s = -7$ $(r)(s) = 6$	$x = 1$ $x = 6$
f. $r = -6; s = -1$ $(2x-1)(x-3) = 2x^2$ $-6x - x + 3 =$ $2x^2 - 7x + 3$	$r + s = -7$ $(r)(s) = 6$	$x = 1/2$ $x = 3$
g. $r = 20; s = -6$ $(4x-3)(2x+5) =$ $8x^2 + 20x - 6x - 15 =$ $8x^2 + 14x - 15$	$r + s = 14$ $(r)(s) = -120$	$x = 3/4$ $x = -5/2$

Expression	r and s	Factor
h. $x^2 - x - 6$	$r + s = -1$ $(r)(s) = -6$ $r = -3; s = 2$	$x^2 - 3x + 2x - 6$ $x(x-3) + 2(x-3)$ $(x+2)(x-3)$
i. $x^2 + 3x - 4$	$r + s = 3$ $(r)(s) = -4$ $r = -1; s = 4$	$x^2 - x + 4x - 4$ $x(x-1) + 4(x-1)$ $(x+4)(x-1)$
j. $x^2 + 6x + 8$	$r + s = 6$ $(r)(s) = 8$ $r = 4; s = 2$	$x^2 + 4x + 2x + 8$ $x(x+4) + 2(x+4)$ $(x+2)(x+4)$
k. $x^2 - 5x + 6$	$r + s = -5$ $(r)(s) = 6$ $r = -3; x = -2$	$x^2 - 3x - 2x + 6$ $x(x-3) - 2(x-3)$ $(x-2)(x-3)$
l. $x^2 - 7x + 6$	$r + s = -7$ $(r)(s) = 6$ $r = -6; s = -1$	$x^2 - 6x - x + 6$ $x(x-6) - 1(x-6)$ $(x-1)(x-6)$
m. $2x^2 - 7x + 3$	$r + s = -7$ $(r)(s) = 6$ $r = -6; s = -1$	$2x^2 - 6x - x + 3$ $x(2x-1) - 3(2x-1)$ $(x-3)(2x-1)$
n. $8x^2 + 14x - 15$	$r + s = 14$ $(r)(s) = -120$ $r = 20; s = -6$	$8x^2 + 20x - 6x - 15$ $4x(2x+5) - 3(2x+5)$ $(4x-3)(2x+5)$

o. $(2x-5)(3x+1) = 0;$ 5/2, –1/3
p. $(4x-2)(x-3) = 0;$ ½, 3
q. $(2x+3)(2x-3) = 0;$ –3/2, 3/2
r. $(2x+3)(2x+3) = 0;$ –3/2

Page 183
   a. 3/2, –5/2
   b. –2/3, –1/4
   c. 2/11, 3
   d. 4/3, –7/2
   e. 3/2, 5/9
   f. 4/9, –2

Page 193
   a. $d = -16t^2 + 25t - 50$ **c.** $0 = -16(1)^2 + v(1) - 50$
   $d = -16t^2 + 50t - 50$ $0 = -16 + v - 50$
   $d = -16t^2 + 75t - 50$ $v = 66 \text{ft/sec}$
   $d = -16t^2 + 100t - 50$

   b. $d = -16t^2 + 25t - 50$; No solutions.
   Does not escape canyon.
   $d = -16t^2 + 50t - 50$; No solutions.
   Does not escape canyon.
   $d = -16t^2 + 75t - 50$;
   Escapes canyon.
   $d = -16t^2 + 100t - 50$; Two solutions.
   Escapes canyon.

Answer Key *(cont.)*

Page 198
Part I.

Paper		Calculator		
Folds	Layers	ENTER	Answer	Power of 2
0	1	0	1	2^0
1	2	1	2	2^1
2	4	2	4	2^2
3	8	3	8	2^3
4	16	4	16	2^4
5	32	5	32	2^5
6	64	6	64	2^6
7	128	7	128	2^7
8	256	8	256	2^8
9	512	9	512	2^9
10	1,024	10	1,024	2^{10}
11	2,048	11	2,048	2^{11}
12	4,096	12	4,096	2^{12}
		x		2^x

Part II.

Year	Dollars	Year	Dollars
0	100	5	131.82
1	106	6	141.85
2	112.36	7	150.36
3	119.11		
4	126.25		

Part III.
Answers may vary.

Page 199
  a. $y = 2^x$; \$268,435,456

  b. $y = 2^{\frac{x}{7}}$; \$256
  c. $3000(1 + .025)5$;
     $3000(1 + .05)^5$;
     \$434.62

Pages 206–207
  I.

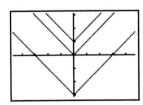

  a. (0, 0)
  b. (0, 1)
  c. (0, –3)

II.
  d. (0, –10)
  e. (0, 25)
  f. A + moves up and a – moves down.
III.

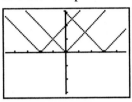

  g. (0, 0)
  h. (3, 0)
  i. (–2, 0)
IV.
  j. (10, 0)
  k. (–25, 0)
  l. + goes left, – goes right.
  V. (7, 2); (–7, –2)
     (–7, 2); (7, –2)
VI. c, up, down, b, left, right.
VII.

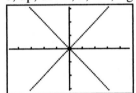

  m. The graphs fit on top of each other.
Pages 208–209
  a. (3, –4)

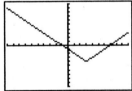

  b. (3, –4)

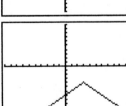

  c. (–2, .5)

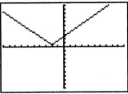

  d. (–2, .5)

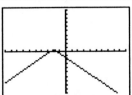

Pages 208–209 *(cont.)*

  e. (0, 0)

  f. (0, 1) up 1; (0, –2) down 2

  g.

Equation	Vertex	Horizontal Shift
$y = x^2$	(0, 0)	none
$y = (x - 2)^2$	(2, 0)	2 right
$y = (x + 3)^2$	(–3, 0)	3 left

  h.

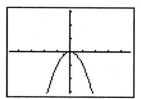

  i.

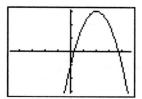

#50024—Graphing Calculator Strategies, Algebra   © *Shell Education*